The Living Wage

The Economy | Key Ideas

These short primers introduce students to the core concepts, theories and models, both new and established, heterodox and mainstream, contested and accepted, used by economists and political economists to understand and explain the workings of the economy.

Published

Behavioural Economics
Graham Mallard

The Living Wage
Donald Hirsch and Laura Valadez-Martinez

The Living Wage

Donald Hirsch
and
Laura Valadez-Martinez

agenda
publishing

First published in 2017 by Agenda Publishing

Agenda Publishing Limited
The Core
Science Central
Bath Lane
Newcastle upon Tyne
NE4 5TF
www.agendapub.com

ISBN 978-1-911116-45-5 (hardcover)
ISBN 978-1-911116-46-2 (paperback)

British Library Cataloguing-in-Publication Data
A catalogue record for this book is available from the British Library

Typeset by JS Typesetting Ltd, Porthcawl, Mid Glamorgan
Printed and bound in the UK by CPI Group (UK) Ltd, Croydon, CR0 4YY

Contents

Preface

The concept of a "living wage", originally a response to the appalling pay and conditions of nineteenth-century sweatshops, has enjoyed a remarkable resurgence in the early twenty-first century. In the United States and the United Kingdom in particular, grassroots movements protesting against a growing pay divide have taken up the cause of a living wage, arguing that paying workers less than they need to live on is both immoral and short-sighted. It is immoral, they say, because workers deserve a fair share of the prosperity to which they contribute, at least at a level that allows them to live in dignity. It is short-sighted because it treats workers as expendable, whereas employees who feel valued show greater loyalty to their employers, and give more value back.

As part of a more general protest against the consequences of present-day capitalism, living wage campaigns have made a lot of noise. But what distinguishes them particularly is their impact. In English-speaking countries, where campaigns have been strongest, millions of workers are getting substantial pay rises under the living wage banner. In the United States, a call for a $15 an hour living wage, over twice the federal minimum, once seemed utopian. Now, California and New York have legislated a $15 minimum, to be phased in over the next few years. In the United Kingdom, the Conservative Party, which had opposed any form of minimum wage until 2000, fifteen years later introduced a "National Living Wage", set to increase the compulsory minimum by 38 per cent for workers over 25. Thousands of companies in the UK, ranging from Ikea to Nestlé, have adopted a higher, voluntary living wage. And living wage campaigns are being extended across the world, urging multinational companies to assure decent pay for manufacturing workers in poorer countries, particularly through supply-chain agreements.

So the idea of a living wage has allowed multiple campaigners to unify around an apparently simple idea and make a real difference to people's lives. Yet its exact meaning, measurement and implementation have been far from uniform. In fact, things called "living wages" have taken so many different forms that to speak of "*the* living wage" is itself an oversimplification (but one that this book occasionally indulges in, when referring to living wage movements as a whole). Moreover, the role of wages in combating poverty is not straightforward: an hourly wage rate is only one of many factors that influence whether households have sufficient income to live a decent life.

This book seeks to give the reader a better understanding of the living wage phenomenon. After tracing the fascinating history of living wages in Chapter 1, it sets out in Chapter 2 how living wages are being interpreted, calculated and applied today, in a range of countries and particularly the United Kingdom and the United States, where campaigns have been the most active. Chapter 3 then looks at the impact on labour markets of setting wages at a minimum level, and Chapter 4 at how living wages can interact with other measures in securing adequate living standards for lower-paid workers and their families. Chapter 5 looks at some issues, dilemmas and choices that the living wage now poses for societies who have accepted its overall desirability, and looks ahead to its possible future.

At one level, the book is an explainer. It assumes that people interested in the living wage would like to know what it really means in practice. What is the difference between a minimum and a living wage? What kind of living standard does a living wage represent? How have strategies for its adoption differed across countries? And what have economists had to say about fixing a lower limit to pay, rather than letting the market determine the price of labour?

Yet this book also tries to provoke thinking about some wider issues that arise from the idea of a living wage. The story of how societies have thought for centuries about fair or adequate pay is a useful introduction to this. Past justifications of minimum pay levels, whether as a moral right or as an economic prerequisite to a well-functioning labour force, have great salience to our present times. Modern advocates often argue that adopting a living wage is a "win–win" – a moral act that also brings prosperity – but this book points to ways in which it can create winners and losers, suggesting that it also needs to be justified in terms of these outcomes being desirable. Furthermore, we argue that the sustainability of living wages may in future depend crucially on other forms of economic and social support for families on low incomes. Without a willingness by governments and their taxpayers to give this support, there may be no guarantee that wages can be set at a level that truly meets people's needs, which employers can afford to pay. Such issues play out differently in different countries, and will do in an uncertain future. Rather than give a single prescription, this book invites readers to think critically about what a living wage really means, and not simply to embrace it as a fuzzy ideal.

Acknowledgements

We are grateful to Alison Howson at Agenda Publishing, for her original suggestion to write this book and for her invaluable support and advice throughout. We greatly appreciated the constructive suggestions on the first draft made by Matt Dickson at the University of Bath. Professor Stephanie Luce of City University of New York gave valuable comments both on the outline and on the manuscript, which helped point us in useful directions.

We also want to express our thanks to all of our team at the Centre for Research in Social Policy (CRSP) at Loughborough University, for carrying out the research that underpins the UK Living Wage, and which has been so fundamental to thinking in this field. Nicola Lomax at CRSP and our production editor Hamish Ironside ably formatted the graphs and diagrams appearing in this book.

A note on terminology

Two key concepts in this book are *living wage* and *minimum wage*. A living wage refers to an hourly rate of pay considered sufficient to produce an acceptable standard of living. A minimum wage refers to a compulsory minimum pay rate. Box 1.1 on page 14 discusses this distinction further, including the fluidity with which people have used these terms.

A *wage floor* is a single term referring to any case where it has been agreed not to let wages drop below a given level – whether through a commitment to pay a living wage or by laws enforcing minimum wages. Chapter 3 considers the economic effects of such wage floors, where they may override a pure market negotiation between employee and employer.

A *subsistence wage* is sometimes used to describe pay sufficient to cover only the bare physical essentials of life, which may be less than what society considers a minimum decent living standard, although some economists use "subsistence" to include anything considered to be necessary by society.

A *minimum income standard* is a way of expressing the income needed for a household to reach a standard of living considered by society to be the minimum that is required. Box 2.2 on page 30 gives a specific example of how this can be measured.

A *Living Wage Ordinance* (United States) is a requirement set by a public body such as a city government, imposing a minimum wage rate on organizations to which it gives money, for example through a service contract or a grant (see page 38).

The *National Living Wage* (United Kingdom) is a higher compulsory minimum wage for workers over 25, introduced in 2016 with the intention of making wages more adequate to live on, but not specifically linked to living costs (see page 23).

The *accredited living wage* (United Kingdom) is a wage rate calculated with reference to the cost of reaching a minimum standard of living.

Employers who commit to paying this wage are recognized by the Living Wage Foundation as Living Wage Employers (see page 41).

Personal *tax credits* are regular payments made by some governments to working families with low incomes. Despite their name, they may be only loosely linked to the tax system; even families not paying tax may be eligible. As with out-of-work benefits, entitlements are related to family composition, with larger families getting more to reflect their greater need. These tax credits are phased out as income rises above a certain level (see page 85).

1

The meaning, origins and development of a living wage

Introduction

A living wage is a concept that overlays a market transaction with a social meaning. At one level, a wage is simply the negotiated price attached to the selling of labour by an employee to an employer – part of an agreed exchange like the price paid for eggs or automobiles. Yet the notion of a "living" wage reminds us of a social aspect of this transaction – whether it allows employees and their dependants to reach an adequate standard of living.

The price of labour is also of interest to society because it can reflect the division of economic power. The shares of national income that accrue to labour and to capital, as well as the distribution of wages between higher and lower paid workers, have varied considerably over time. Classical economic theory says that these shares will be determined by the laws of supply and demand, with the price of various "factors of production" (land, labour and capital) partly reflecting their relative scarcity. In practice, they are also affected by a host of imperfections in markets, including unequal negotiating positions of different parties. In some cases, such as a well-organized trade union threatening to call a strike, this may potentially favour workers; in others, such as boardroom executives setting the pay of their peers or distributing profits to favour the better-off, it may help divert resources to managers or to shareholders.

Ever since the advent of wage labour, therefore, two fundamental questions have arisen for ordinary employees: are wages fair, and are they enough for a worker to subsist? These questions overlap, but are not identical. The issue of fairness may relate to whether a wage reflects the true value of a worker's labour, a difficult to assess, somewhat abstract concept. A more concrete issue is whether the wage is enough to subsist at an acceptable level.

A living wage is one that is adequate for a worker to live on. This is the core concept behind a living wage, although it immediately raises a host of issues including what we mean by adequate, how many hours someone should have to work and the extent to which the wage should cover dependants – issues that will be addressed in this book.

Wages below an adequate level, produced by market transactions, can be problematic, for individuals, society and ultimately the economy. For individuals, they can produce poverty and hardship. For society, this can have knock-on effects, including for example high rates of illness or disease, or social unrest. For the economy, productivity may be damaged by the poor quality of labour that tends to be given by underpaid people living in hardship.

All these factors make it hard to disagree that workers should at least be paid a living wage. What is harder to say is exactly how such a wage should be calculated, and how it should be achieved in a market economy.

This book considers how living wages are being interpreted, advocated and implemented, and looks at a range of issues surrounding their implementation. First, however, this chapter looks at the history of living wages, and at how the ideas behind them have evolved to the present day.

Morality, rights and economic sustainability: the evolution of the living wage in thinking and practice

In modern societies, wage labour has for most people replaced other ways of translating work into survival – such as self-sufficiency, barter, feudal/family obligations and self-employment. Ever since wage labour emerged, the question has arisen of whether workers are paid enough to make a living. A centuries-old dialogue about living wages has involved religious thinkers and philosophers considering what is moral; and economic thinkers considering what brings prosperity. A striking aspect of this dialogue is how often moral and economic reasoning have been used to reinforce each other rather than being in conflict, often with a single thinker having both of these aspects in mind.

The following selective account traces how the idea of a just or living wage evolved, how the concept has interacted with economic developments of different times and how ideas have been translated into practice.

The medieval just price

In late medieval Europe, feudal duties and non-monetary forms of exchange started to be replaced by market transactions including wage labour. This transition from a system of well-understood obligations to the largely amoral workings of the market caused understandable concern that prices would unduly upset the economic order. Theologians such as Thomas Aquinas taught that prices should be "just", by which he meant that they should follow the Christian teaching of taking into account other people's needs. This meant that, as a minimum, both the seller and the buyer should be assured a livelihood. While markets could be used to determine the price within these constraints, it was considered immoral to make unfair use of unequal market power (see Stabile 2008: 15). There was also a strong concept of a "normal and customary" price from which it was wrong to depart, advocated for example by the early economic thinker Bernardino of Siena. Christian writers of this time did not deny the role of the market in determining the normal price, but considered virtuous economic behaviour to exclude taking undue advantage of a favourable market position.

It is interesting to note that one of the most important early interventions to curb what was considered unfairness in labour markets was to legislate not for a minimum wage but for a maximum wage. In the wake of the Black Death, the shortage of labour in England was enabling peasants to leave the lands to which they had been tied through the feudal system, and to demand relatively high wages elsewhere. The Statute of Labourers, passed in 1351, decreed a maximum wage and attempted to prevent workers from moving around. This prompted the unsuccessful Peasants' Revolt. In the centuries that followed, similar laws allowed local magistrates and guilds to regulate wages in particular trades, sometimes setting minimum and sometimes maximum levels, but to a large degree defending the interests of employers rather than workers. However, in an early demonstration that regulation cannot easily push against market forces, it proved hard in the middle ages to prevent agricultural wages from rising in response to falling population: they roughly doubled in the century following the original Statute of Labourers. On the other hand, after population started increasing in the sixteenth century, real wages fell sharply, and despite advances in agriculture, by the 1860s they were no higher than at the time of the Peasants' Revolt (Clark 2007).

ARTICULATING THE LIVING WAGE: PRE-INDUSTRIAL SOCIETY

Key concept

- The language of *equitable* wages in this period emphasized fairness and justice.

What they said

Merit and reward refer to the same, for a reward means something given anyone in return for work or toil, as a price for it. Hence, as it is an act of justice to give a just price for anything received from another, so also is it an act of justice to make a return for work or toil.   Aquinas (1265–74)

For the worker is worth his keep.   Matthew 10.10

Classical economics and faith in markets

If medieval church thinkers felt that market behaviour must be bounded by Christian faith, modern economists felt rather that we should have faith in markets, to produce the best outcomes. In particular, Adam Smith, the "father of economics", argued that markets rather than individual morality were the route to collective prosperity in the modern world. He was writing in the late eighteenth century, when urbanization and industrialization were making it much harder to be guided by what Smith called the "moral economy": well understood social and economic relationships that worked best in small-scale, stable communities. While the Christian principle of taking account of the needs of others was still valid, it could not guide all economic transactions.

Smith believed that a freely functioning market would produce the desirable result of ensuring that workers would achieve a subsistence wage. Unlike some people using the term "subsistence" to describe the bare means of survival, Smith used it to mean providing "necessaries":

By necessaries I understand, not only the commodities which are indispensably necessary for the support of life, but whatever the custom of the country renders it indecent for creditable people, even of the lowest order, to be without.   (Smith 1776: 479)

This shows that the idea of a living wage needing to be seen in relation to the way people live in a particular country at a particular time, rather than judged by an absolute standard, is nothing new.

Smith believed that free markets worked to keep wages at or above such a level (other than in declining industries that were being replaced by more viable ones), and indeed to increase what this minimum entailed, by raising general prosperity. He argued that if wages fell below subsistence, the supply of labour would be undermined as workers may choose to beg or steal to make ends meet, while a sufficient wage helped maintain workers in a capable state. In other words, adequate wages enhance both the quality and the quantity of the labour supply, making employers willing to pay such wages. He also observed that interference with markets tended in his time to have the malign effect of keeping wages down (such as through agreements within a trade to cap wages), since those in power were still generally on the side of the "masters". Hence deregulation of labour markets was in Smith's view the best route to a living wage.

Thus the dawn of modern economics saw strong support for a living wage, but confidence that it could best be achieved by letting markets work unhampered. Other early economic thinkers such as the philosopher John Stuart Mill agreed with Smith about the importance of maintaining wages at least at an adequate level, although another early economist, Robert Malthus, was more gloomy about the long-term effects of rising productivity, believing that it would always lead to population expansion, which kept workers at a low level of subsistence. While Mill supported Smith's view opposing regulation enabling employers to restricting wages, he proposed that free markets may not be enough to redress the balance in favour of employees without individual workers combining into trade unions (Mill [1909] 1969: 933–4).

The early economists therefore emphasized the benefits of people pursuing their interests freely in market transactions, in contrast to the medieval reliance on moral behaviour. Yet unlike free market economists today, Adam Smith and his successors attached great economic importance to wages being adequate. They were concerned with the collective capabilities of labour, and the part that wage levels play in this. Perhaps because so many workers at the time were at the margins of physical subsistence, they connected worker well-being and living standards with the productive potential of labour. Even the production of future workers, through procreation, was seen to be affected by the well-being of today's employees. Thus, adequate wage levels were linked closely to economic sustainability and future growth. Current prevailing economic theory, on the other hand, considers workers much more as individuals, starting with the principle that wages are determined by the "marginal product of labour". This means that an employer will hire an additional worker only if someone is willing to accept a job at an hourly wage no greater than the value of what they can produce in an hour (minus any other costs of hiring them). A market system that considers wages only in this context makes no reference to consequences for living standards or for the aggregate effect on labour supply of how wage levels compare to workers' basic needs.

The crusade for living wages in the late nineteenth- and early twentieth centuries

As the industrial revolution progressed, it became ever harder to agree with Adam Smith's assessment that markets could be relied upon to bring workers to a living standard that met their basic needs. Describing conditions in the "sweatshops" of East London in the 1880s, the social reformer Beatrice Webb cited a chilling report from a parliamentary committee:

> These evils can scarcely be exaggerated ... earnings barely sufficient to sustain existence; hours of labour such as to make the lives of the workers periods of almost ceaseless toil, hard and unlovely to the last degree; sanitary conditions injurious to the health of the persons employed and dangerous to the public.
>
> (Select Committee of the House of Lords on the Sweating System 1888–9: xlii, xliii)

The asymmetry of power between employers and their workers, already acknowledged by Smith, was not proving easy to correct. In Karl Marx's view, it was endemic to capitalism, since employers held property and workers were constrained to sell their labour in order to survive (Marx [1885] 1977: 769). Moreover, in a growing economy, Marx saw "subsistence" as a changing concept, since social satisfaction is relative to the norms of the society one lives in, so as society prospers, people need more (Marx [1849]

CLASSICAL ECONOMISTS SEE SUFFICIENT WAGES AS FUNDAMENTAL TO SUSTAIN LABOUR

Key concept

- *Invisible hand:* this is a concept used by Adam Smith, meaning the principle that rational economic actors pursuing their own self-interest in free markets will produce the best possible social results, by maximizing prosperity – since markets and prices ensure the most efficient deployment of resources. In the case of labour, sufficient wages would be achieved through such market forces. A wage too low to sustain workers would damage the supply of effective labour (by causing people not to work, or by reducing their capacity to work efficiently) – and in the light of this shortage, employers would be willing to pay more to secure capable workers, causing the wage rate to rise until it reached the required level of subsistence and the shortage disappeared.

What they said

A man must always live by his work, and his wages must at least be sufficient to maintain him. They must even upon most occasions be somewhat more; otherwise it would be impossible for him to bring up a family, and the race of such workmen could not last beyond the first generation. Adam Smith (1776: 46)

Where wages are high, accordingly, we shall always find the workmen more active, diligent, and expeditious than where they are low.
Adam Smith (*ibid.*: 53)

[H]ealth and strength, physical, mental and moral, are the basis of industrial efficiency, on which the production of material wealth depends, while conversely, the chief importance of material wealth lies in the fact that, when used wisely, it increases the health and strength, physical mental and moral, of the human race. Alfred Marshall (1895: 274)

1972: 180). Yet workers were hampered in keeping up with these changing norms, since Marx concluded that capitalists would always appropriate most of the fruits of growth to pursue "luxuries". This view regarded capitalists as prospering from the exploitation of labour, and therefore more adequate wages as something that bosses would resist, rather than see as making a contribution to general prosperity.

While Marx advocated an overthrow of a system governed by markets, reformers looked for ways of securing acceptable living standards for workers within a market system. The last two decades of the nineteenth- and first two decades of the twentieth centuries saw an outpouring of reforming zeal among those who thought that morality and markets could and should be reconciled.

In these years, a living wage was explicitly advocated by reformers on both sides of the Atlantic. These reformers came from diverse backgrounds, from theologians such as the leading US Catholic thinker John Augustus Ryan to philanthropic industrialists such as the Yorkshire wool manufacturer Mark Oldroyd and the chocolate-making Rowntrees, as well as the socialist reformer Beatrice Webb. While the arguments and proposals put by these reformers were diverse, they shared important common threads.

In particular, while outraged by the miserable conditions of many workers and often asserting a living wage as a basic "right", reformers of this era did not see decent pay merely in terms of charity or philanthropy. Rather, they saw it as a precondition of on the one hand industrial efficiency, and on the other individual self-realization. In terms of efficiency, they repeated classical economists' view that decent living conditions were needed for an efficient labour force. In terms of self-realization, they argued that enabling people to support themselves through work would both allow them to function as citizens and be good for them morally by allowing self-reliance. This reflected a fundamental change from the traditional, pre-industrial idea of a just price based on the natural order of things. In these later times, the emphasis was on individuals and their fulfilment through moral behaviour. Having the opportunity to earn a wage that you could live on encouraged personal responsibility, and reformers such as Charles Booth (1889) favoured stern supervision in labour colonies of "loafers" who did not take up these opportunities. In the United States, moreover, being able to function as an independent citizen from an economic perspective was associated, in the relatively young republic, with having political independence (Levin-Waldman 2005: 21).

Another important feature of the reformers of this time is that they were devoted to science. Not only did they meticulously document the conditions of working people, but they carefully researched their needs. In York,

Seebohm Rowntree (1901) made a detailed study of the cost of food, clothing and other necessities that a man would need to provide for a family with three children, and used the results to advocate a weekly wage of 35 shillings and three pence in 1914.

REFORMING ZEAL: EARLY ARGUMENTS FOR A LIVING WAGE

Key concepts

- The living wage articulated for the first time as a right.
- Emerging political movements: socialism, co-operativism, trade unionism.
- Self-reliance, and the obligation to earn one's living.
- In the United States, individual economic independence, tied to national political independence.

What they said

A living wage must be sufficient to maintain the worker in the highest state of industrial efficiency, with decent surroundings and sufficient leisure.   Mark Oldroyd, industrialist (Oldroyd 1894: 8)

The primary natural right from which the right to a Living Wage is deduced, is the right to subsist upon the bounty of the earth.
Father John Ryan, Catholic priest (Ryan 1912: 68)

On account of his sacredness as a person, every member of a community has an abstract right to a decent livelihood ... Now, the simple and sufficient reason why this general right of the laborer takes the special form of a right to a Living Wage, is that in the present industrial organization of society, there is no other way in which the right can be realized.
Father John Ryan (*ibid.*: 37)

Let the working man and the employer make free agreements, and in particular let them agree freely as to the wages; nevertheless, there underlies a dictate of natural justice more imperious and ancient than any bargain between man and man, namely, that wages ought not to be insufficient to support a frugal and well-behaved wage-earner.
Pope Leo XIII (Leo 1891)

Twentieth-century directions: collective bargaining and wage floors

Early advocates of living wages all wanted manual workers to be paid enough to live on, but they had different visions of how this should be achieved. Some called for a general wage "floor" which all employers were required to pay as a minimum (in many cases, though, not recommending this for women, since the emphasis was on men supporting families). Some wanted to apply it more selectively to different trades. Others emphasized collective bargaining between trade unions and individual employers. During the twentieth century, each of these three methods of wage setting was put into practice at different times and in different ways.

Among reformers supporting a legal minimum, there was a distinction between those calling for an enforced "living wage" and those advocating "minimum wages". In the UK in the 1890s, for example, the radical economist J. A. Hobson suggested that a living wage allowing for a decent living standard including leisure was a feasible way of giving workers a just share of wealth. Less ambitiously, Sidney and Beatrice Webb proposed a legislated minimum wage providing only for basic subsistence, as an extension of factory acts that regulated working hours and conditions. The latter approach was part of the "anti-sweating" movement (opposing industrial "sweatshops" with appalling conditions), which focused on trades with the worst pay, hours and conditions. The Webbs called such wages "parasitic", because their workers could only survive with the help of charity from the rest of society (see Blackburn 2007).

The first minimum wages were introduced in New Zealand (1894) and the Australian state of Victoria (1896), initially covering selected trades through arbitration courts, but soon evolving into national legal minimums. While they originated in the anti-sweating movement and thus aimed to end wages too low to subsist on, Australia came closest in this period to pursuing a more ambitious "living wage". In 1907, in the landmark *Harvester* case, a judged affirmed that wages must cover "the normal needs of an average employee, regarded as a human being in a civilized community". This set a precedent for a generous minimum wage level in Australia – which even today is the highest in the world, according to OECD data, at just over US$15 an hour at prevailing exchange rates in 2015.

In other countries, even achieving a more basic minimum proved an uphill battle, faced with the power of industrial interests who opposed any interference in labour markets. In the UK, after a long struggle, very selective protection in certain low-paid industries was legislated by the reforming Liberal government in 1909, in the Trades Boards Act. The boards set different minimum wage levels in each industry, negotiated by worker and employer representatives and independent members. While the trade boards and their successors, the wages councils, lasted until 1993, wages in the industries covered tended to stay low, in contrast to others covered by strong unions, bargaining directly with employers. Arguably, this watered down version of minimum pay contributed to the failure of the UK to introduce a national minimum wage until 1999.

In the United States several states adopted minimum ages in the early twentieth century, and a national minimum was introduced by Roosevelt's New Deal government in the 1930s. An initial version was thrown out by the Supreme Court because it exceeded federal power to regulate state commerce, but a later version was upheld. Roosevelt explicitly intended the minimum to be "more than a bare subsistence level" saying it should represent "the wages of a decent living", although in later years the federal minimum wage increasingly came to be seen as a barely sufficient rate of pay. States, and some cities within them, are allowed to set their own, higher minimum, and today most states do. In Europe, many countries have tended to rely to a large degree on collective agreements of wage rates between unions and employers in each sector, but a national minimum was introduced in the Netherlands in 1969, France in 1970 and Spain in 1980. In Germany, for reasons discussed below, the first national minimum was only introduced in 2015. Countries such as Denmark, Finland and Norway still have no national minimum, but collective agreements are legally binding.

In practice, the achievement of improved wages in the twentieth century owed much more to collective bargaining between trade unions and employers than to the setting of national minimum wages. As we have seen, some bargaining was carried out systematically by sector, and some was legally binding; on the other hand in the UK in particular, most bargaining agreements were voluntary deals between unions and employers, with the state or the law playing no explicit role. Trade unions in this context tended to be cautious about, or even resistant to, the idea of a national minimum wage. The most successful unions had negotiated wages well above what any general minimum was likely to be, and feared that a focus on such a minimum might reduce their influence, or narrow pay differentials which

PRACTICAL IMPLEMENTATION: MINIMUM WAGES AND COLLECTIVE BARGAINING

Key concepts

- *Minimum wage*: a legal minimum, usually covering all jobs, although sometimes with exemptions.
- *Collective bargaining*: pay negotiations between trade unions as agreed representatives of workers, and an employer or the representatives of employers within one sector.
- *Collective agreement*: the setting of wages across a sector or occupation, sometimes legally binding.

What they said

> [A subsistence minimum wage] … means that people are not paid what they are worth but what is necessary to keep them working. That is how the horse or slave is paid.
> R. H. Tawney (cited in Winter & Joslin 1972: 48)

> It is a serious national evil that any class of His Majesty's subjects should receive less than a living wage in return for their utmost exertions. It was formerly supposed that the working of the laws of supply and demand would naturally regulate or eliminate that evil [and] ultimately produce a fair price. Where … you have a powerful organisation on both sides … there you have a healthy bargaining … But where you have what we call sweated trades, you have no organisation, no parity of bargaining, the good employer is undercut by the bad, and the bad employer is undercut by the worst … where those conditions prevail you have not a condition of progress, but a condition of progressive degeneration.
> Winston Churchill, President of Board of Trade,
> introducing Trades Boards Bill (1909)

> No business which depends for existence on paying less than living wages to its workers has any right to continue in this country.
> Franklin D. Roosevelt (1933)

> All statutory methods of wage fixing and other conditions of employ-ment are by the law itself considered as a second best. All British labour legislation is, in a sense a gloss or footnote to collective bargaining.
> Otto Kahn-Freund (1968: 32)

their members had an interest in preserving. They could also see that when bargaining was subject to a legal negotiation through a public body (a trade board or a wages council), it had often not been as effective as when a union was negotiating directly for its members, with the ultimate sanction of strike action.

Recent transitions: a weakening of collective bargaining and the renewed quest for living wages

In most industrialized countries, the membership of trade unions has declined sharply since the 1970s, as have the conditions in which they thrived. These trends are partly the result of a change in the shape of the workforce: much fewer workers are in industries such as large-scale man-ufacturing, mining and services provided directly by state employees, in which labour is most easily organized. More people work in private service industries. Perhaps just as importantly, worker negotiation of pay has been affected by a more competitive, global economic environment. Collective bargaining has become more difficult in the face of greater competition in product markets, because employers feel they have less room to compro-mise with workers negotiating higher wages, which may add to costs and to prices. In addition, some countries have weakened the rights of trade unions in their labour laws. One important trend has been the privatization of jobs previously performed directly by public sector workers but now by those working for private contractors selling services to governments. In these sectors, companies competing for contracts are less inclined to agree pay rises that might make their bids less competitive, and are often not unionized (see Brown *et al.* 2008). Meanwhile, the weakening of job secu-rity and the growth of work supplied as a series of one-off arrangements (the so-called "gig economy" – see page 98 below) pose further challenges to workers' bargaining position.

Recent movements for improved minimum wages and for living wages can be seen against the background of this changed world. The heyday of collective bargaining has passed, and the vast majority of workers are unlikely to benefit from it, if only because they do not belong to a union. At the same time, the state has not obviously stepped in to improve protection: the fall in union membership in the United States has been paralleled by a fall in the real value of the federal minimum wage (Box 1.1).

BOX 1.1 A CHANGE IN DISCOURSE: FROM UNION POWER TO THE REAL VALUE OF MINIMUM WAGES IN THE UNITED STATES

While three out of ten workers were unionized in the 1960s, only one out of ten workers is a member of a union in the United States today. This decline in union membership means that the fight for higher wages has become disassociated from collective bargaining, opening up the route for new dialogues between workers, employers and the government.

At the heart of the new discourse is the fact that the federal minimum wage has fallen in real value since the 1960s, at the same time as workers have on average become twice as productive. As shown in Figure 1.1, only a small amount of these productivity gains have translated into higher average wages, but workers on the minimum have done especially badly.

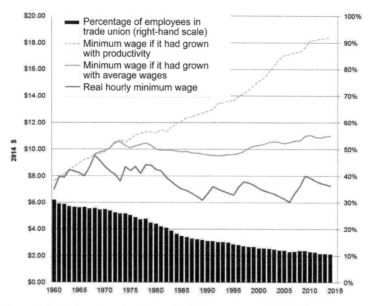

Figure 1.1 Trade union density and minimum wages, United States 1960–2015.

Sources: OECD; Economic Policy Institute; US Bureau of Labor Statistics; authors' calculations

In this changed environment, minimum and living wages are being looked at in new ways in a range of countries.

In the United States, there is increasing political focus on raising the federal minimum wage, which by 2016 had not increased for seven years. Elsewhere, labour movements that once appeared committed to established forms of collective bargaining have come to see a general minimum as being more important than previously, for example in the United Kingdom and Germany.

In the UK, both the Labour Party and much of the trade union movement moved from wariness to wholehearted support of a national minimum wage, which was introduced by a Labour government in 1999. Its popularity meant that opposition by Labour's main opponents, the Conservatives, eventually melted away, and as we shall see in Chapter 4, the Conservatives now present themselves as champions of a higher legal minimum.

In Germany, the commitment to set wages only through collective bargaining lasted longer, but coverage of such agreements has now declined, from the great majority of workers to only just over half. This eventually persuaded the Social Democrat Party to support a statutory minimum, reluctantly agreed by their coalition partners, the conservative Christian Democrats, and implemented in 2015.

Yet it is not just the need for a compulsory wage "floor", but also its level, that is being brought into question. In the United States, the 17 per cent decline of the federal minimum since 1970 means that it is increasingly associated with working poverty, and Franklin D. Roosevelt's association of a minimum wage with a living wage seems a distant memory. In the UK, the national minimum wage was introduced at a cautious level, and increases are negotiated between employers, trade unions and independent economists – but without reference to minimum living standards.

The re-emergence of living wage campaigns has in part been a challenge to inadequate minimum wages. This is a revival of the debates of the 1890s about whether a minimum should just seek to prevent exploitative low rates of pay by rogue employers – or whether more ambitiously it should be designed to ensure that workers reach decent living standards. Much of the language of living wage movements in countries such as the United States, the United Kingdom and New Zealand in the past 20 years has echoes of these earlier debates. This refers to the dignity of workers, their ability to meet the needs of their families and to the ethics of leaving some workers in need while others live in luxury. Also in common with previous movements, living wage campaigns draw both on Christian activists and social reformers for inspiration, and focus their efforts on particular areas of the workforce where pay is lowest.

However, current movements are also distinct from those of the past in important respects. They generally do not emanate from thinkers and writers but from local activists. These "bottom-up" campaigns bring together new types of coalition – typically involving local church groups, community organizers and trade unions. Their target is a particular form of injustice, centring round the decline in jobs, security and pay in a post-industrial economy. And their ambitions are also tailored to the modern world. The most fruitful target in the United States has been public sector contracting: securing the agreement of city governments to require those accepting public money to pay a living wage. In the United Kingdom, the London Living Wage campaign started with the public shaming of large, wealthy employers who were under-paying their cleaners. These are different starting points from the sweatshop manufacturers of the industrial revolution, and reflect what campaigners see as going wrong in the twenty-first century.

A further consequence of a modern view is that it is ultimately internationalist. Globalization means that the sweatshops of Bangladesh are tied into the economies of London or New York, where many of their products are worn. After 1,129 Bangladeshis died in garment factories in the Rana Plaza complex when it collapsed in 2013, campaigners from European countries pressed Western clothes manufacturers to adopt an "Asia Floor Wage".

Chapter 2 describes the living wage in the twenty-first century in more detail.

Commentary: what can we learn today from the history of the living wage?

In each era, people calling for a living wage have attached their own meaning to this phrase, and its influence has related to the context of the times. In the late middle ages, as wage labour started to become more common, religious thinkers sought to ensure that fair rewards were maintained. In the early industrial revolution, economists argued that free markets could bring prosperity, and thought that in doing so they could ensure that workers had decent living standards that allowed them to be productive. A century later, reformers responded to the appalling living standards that actually occurred

A MODERN LIVING WAGE MOVEMENT

Key concepts

- *Working poverty:* households who live below the poverty line despite having at least one person in work.
- *Wage inequalities:* the differences in pay between better and worse paid workers, which have generally increased since the 1970s.
- *Corporate social responsibility:* the desire of big businesses to have reputations as acting responsibly towards their workers, customers and society.

What they said

The central argument for the living wage is that, because the economy in general and local economies in particular have failed to generate jobs that pay wages sufficient to support families, minimum (living) wages must be mandated to compensate for this structural failure.

Oren Levin-Waldman (2005: 27)

The [US] living wage movement ... is not simply concerned with improving wages for workers employed by businesses holding municipal government contracts, even though this is the immediate target of their efforts. The living wage movement is committed to reversing the economy-wide wage squeeze, stopping tax giveaways to big business, reenergizing the labor movement, and ending the war on the poor.

Robert Pollin and Stephanie Luce (1998: 7–8)

by arguing for a living wage to restore dignity to workers. While the twentieth century saw a basic minimum to prevent exploitation introduced in many countries, it was growing trade union power and its exercise through collective bargaining that did most to bring working class wages to a level that allowed a decent rather than minimalist living standard. However, a decline in this power in recent years, and changes in labour markets creating growing pay inequalities, have stimulated today's renewed call for a living wage sufficient to allow workers to reach a reasonable standard of living.

Despite such differences in context, this history shows important commonalities relevant to today's debates. One common thread is that wage earners should get a fair share of the fruits of their labour despite unequal economic power. This idea of fairness has owed much to Christian and other ethical arguments that nobody should exploit an advantageous position where this prevents others from meeting their needs. This has been relevant even for free market economists, who have criticized ways in which markets have often been rigged or distorted to favour employers. Today, it is debatable whether markets can really work properly when decisions about the relative pay of bosses and ordinary workers are taken in boardrooms, by those with an interest in keeping executive pay high.

The concept of a living wage, however, goes beyond the idea that labour should not be unfairly exploited, relative to its value. Living wage advocates have argued that regardless of what a worker produces, it is immoral to pay less than what one needs to live in dignity. This has also been a key target of critics of the living wage, arguing that you cannot pay someone more than what they are worth as a worker. One response to this, exemplified by the

---

BOX 1.2 DEFINITIONS: IS THERE ANY CONSISTENT DISTINCTION BETWEEN A LIVING WAGE AND A MINIMUM WAGE?

Writers using these two terms have meant many different things. Yet the prevailing tendency has been to use "living wage" to describe one that delivers an adequate living standard, and "minimum wage" as a national legally binding obligation on employers.

The limitation with these respective definitions is that each addresses a different aspect of wages: their level and their legal status respectively. While minimum wages often make no reference to a living standard, in some cases they do: in the late nineteenth- and early twentieth centuries the term was used by British reformers to argue for a legal minimum allowing basic subsistence, while in the 1930s Roosevelt equated his federal minimum wage with a decent living standard. Conversely, a "living wage" in some cases has comparable legal status to a minimum wage, with some local or national governments using the term to emphasize their intent of setting a legal minimum at a level sufficient for people to live on.

The focus of this book is on people arguing for wages to be set at least at a level that can deliver acceptable minimum living standards. We can think of this broadly as a living wage, but must always be aware that different people use the language of wages in different ways.

---

quote from Franklin D. Roosevelt earlier in this chapter, is that firms have no business creating jobs that people cannot live on.

This debate has always been much deeper than calculations about pay rates: it concerns the position of workers in the economy and society. From Adam Smith to the present day, many have argued that the economy needs workers who are healthy and who themselves prosper. This is partly because they are likely to be more productive, and also because as consumers they will help drive economic growth by generating demand. While a narrow conception of nurturing workers is to ensure that they do not go hungry, R. H. Tawney's remark that a man is not a horse illustrates well the argument for a wage that yields more than survival at a level that allows someone to be a physically efficient worker. By conceiving of a living wage as one that enables workers and their dependants to reach a living standard described by Smith as it being "indecent" to live below according to "the custom of the country", thinkers have recognized that a worker cannot be looked at coldly as a mere "factor of production". Working for a living wage is about being *part* of a prospering society, not just a tool for its creation. The remainder of this book considers how this end is being pursued in the twenty-first century. Chapter 2 starts with a description of how living wages are being calculated, advocated and implemented.

2

Contemporary living wages in practice

Living wage movements have been growing in prominence around the world. This chapter reviews the characteristics, objectives and achievements of these movements. It starts by giving a brief characterization of how they have developed in different countries. The chapter then looks thematically at three key aspects of living wages in practice: how they are calculated, how they are advocated and how they are implemented.

Living wages around the world

Most countries around the world have some form of minimum wage, either general or by industry or occupation. In many countries, there is an implicit aspiration that these wages should be sufficient to allow workers a decent standard of living. However, much fewer countries have explicit "living wages" or living wage campaigns. These have emerged in particular in English-speaking countries in recent years.

United States

Across the United States, hundreds of local living wage campaigns have sprung up since the early 1990s. These campaigns, often driven by community action groups, many supported by faith-based organizations, and also involving trade unions, were typically founded to improve pay for specific groups of low-wage workers in local areas. Such a bottom-up approach has had many different strategies for achieving change. Its most widespread success has been in getting cities to pass ordinances establishing a living wage rate for any employer receiving public contracts to deliver services. Within a decade of the first such ordinance in Baltimore in 1994, over 100 cities had done the same.

The plight of workers providing public services at very low pay rates via contracted employers thus gave impetus to the contemporary US living wage movement, not least because public authorities had leverage over these employers as their clients. However, this revival of the living wage concept, combined with growing wage inequalities and the continuing fall in the value of the federal minimum, has stimulated wider efforts to extend wage floors. Various employers such as corporations, universities and employers within defined areas such as airports have been encouraged to adopt a living wage.

More broadly, campaigns to impose a higher minimum for all employees within cities and states have enjoyed considerable success. As of 2016, 29 states, Washington DC, and at least 36 cities and localities had enacted local minimum wages higher than the federal rate. To a large extent, the living wage movement and demands for a higher minimum wage have become blurred. This has been influenced by a growing "fight for $15" campaign (seeking a minimum over twice the federal rate of $7.25, as of 2016), originating with fast-food workers and their unions and involving the Occupy movement and others. Proposals to raise the federal minimum has also involved high-profile political conflict, with President Obama's proposal to do so being successfully blocked by the Republican-controlled Congress.

More details on the nature and achievements of these US living wage movements are discussed thematically below alongside developments in other countries.

United Kingdom

As in the United States, the United Kingdom has many local living wage campaigns. In contrast, however, there is a single coordinated system for setting a living wage level and accrediting employers who pay it. The movement started in London, with a grassroots organization, London Citizens, arguing that the national minimum wage introduced in 1999 was much too low to cover Londoners' costs, and persuading the Greater London Authority and mayor to support a voluntary London living wage. The movement later spread across the country, with the introduction in 2011 of a coordinated

UK rate (alongside a higher London rate) by the Living Wage Foundation, which had accredited over 3,000 living wage employers by 2017. In that year, the growing popularity of the living wage idea caused the UK government to introduce a substantially higher compulsory minimum wage for over-25s, labelled the National Living Wage. Since this was not systematically based on living costs, unlike the voluntary rate accredited by the Living Wage Foundation, the living wage movement continued to campaign for employers to adopt this "real" rate. From 2016, a Living Wage Commission comprising leading business and union leaders and independent academics established a single system for calculating such a rate, with one figure for London and another for the rest of the UK.

Canada

Living wage movements emerged later in Canada than in the United States. They are furthest ahead in British Columbia, where they were driven by a particular issue in the mid-2000s, namely health care providers contracting out workers, many of whom were mothers supporting families, who immediately lost union status and experienced sharp cuts in pay. Campaigns are highly devolved, each setting their own rate, but in an effort to increase coordination, a single body now publishes a common methodology for calculating local rates. One prominent campaigning group, Living Wage for Families in Vancouver, having persuaded the city government as well as a number of small organizations such as credit unions to become living wage employers, is now seeking to recruit larger private employers in an effort to spread living wages through supply chains. A potential obstacle is that even with a common calculating method, there remains a multiplicity of living wage levels in different communities, leading to an effort to agree common rates for each area type across British Columbia.

New Zealand

Living wage campaigns have developed relatively recently in New Zealand, only becoming established since 2010. To a large degree, they mirror the model in the United Kingdom: local campaigns seeking to persuade employers to adopt a living wage, whose level is set by a national accrediting body, Living Wage Aotearoa NZ. Despite the fact that rents are higher in Auckland, it was decided to adopt a single national rate, and to rely on housing allowances to compensate low income families facing higher rents. By mid-2016, just over 50 New Zealand employers had signed up to the living wage, and a newly elected mayor and council in Wellington favoured making it the first council to pay the living wage to its staff.

Republic of Ireland

Unlike in the United States, and the United Kingdom, where the living wage grew from grassroots campaigns, in Ireland it has been the initiative of think tanks and research institutes with support from trade unions. The Vincentian Partnership for Social Justice, a Catholic charity, promotes active citizenship and the development with citizens of minimum incomes standards using the same method as researchers in the United Kingdom (see Box 2.1 below). In 2014, these results became the basis of the launch of a living wage benchmark by a group of organizations led by the Nevin Economic Research Institute.

Worldwide movements

"The provision of an adequate living wage" has been an objective in the preamble of the International Labour Organization (ILO) since its inception at the Versailles Peace Conference in 1919. Yet in most of the ILO's 187 member states, the definition and implementation of a living wage remains elusive. Nothing resembling a single system for measuring or acknowledging living wages exists at this international level, and multinational companies operating in developing countries have often used this as a reason for not making the payment of a living wage an objective (Anker 2011: 7–8).

Nevertheless, recent moves to develop a global approach to a living wage have focused on the objective of promoting living wages for workers in international supply chains. The impetus for this has come from ethical initiatives in countries that buy cheap goods from the developing world, in particular in Europe. For example, the ACT (Action, Collaboration, Trading) initiative on living wages brings together international brands, retailers, manufacturers and trade unions to address the issue of living wages in the textile and garment supply chain. The initiative seeks to use collective bargaining within industries in a country to agree legally binding living wages that prevent other suppliers from undercutting them. Crucially, it uses purchasing agreements to create incentives for countries to implement such living wages, in the knowledge that this will help them sell their goods to the purchasing companies. In parallel, the Asia Floor Wage alliance proposes a common method for calculating a wage designed to support a common minimum living standard among garment workers in different Asian countries (where most of the world's garments are produced).

How are living wages being calculated?

Many people talk about "a living wage" as though its appropriate level is self-evident. In practice, there is no single way of calculating this level, since there are multiple aspects of a living wage that can be addressed in different ways. In particular, assuming (as most calculations do) that wages need to be considered in terms of supporting households, not just single individuals, the following issues need to be clarified:

- On what basis are households' needs determined?
- What size household does a wage need to support, or contribute to supporting?
- How many hours of work is it expected that people in such a household should work?
- Once calculated, how should a living wage be adjusted over time?

For each of these questions, we consider the range of possible answers, and some examples of how calculations are made in practice.

Determining households' needs

As discussed in Chapter 1, the term "living wage" implies that it is enough to allow a household to reach an acceptable living standard. A first step in calculating it is to specify how much disposable income a family of a particular composition requires (after deducting tax and including any cash benefits) in order to reach such a standard. This typically involves considering minimum budget requirements under various headings, such as food, clothing and leisure. It is also important to include the often considerable costs that enable people to work – particularly the cost of childcare in the case of families with children.

But how can "needs" under each spending category be measured? This is much more than a technical issue, and is at the heart of what a living wage actually represents, with both philosophical and political implications.

At the broadest level, there are four main sources of information about what people *need* in order to have an acceptable life:

- *Expert knowledge.* For example, you need to have certain nutrients in your diet to keep you healthy.
- *Observation* of how people actually live, or what they spend. For example, most people have a television, so being able to afford a television could be seen as a social norm.
- *Public opinion.* For example, members may be asked to judge what norms of living – such as how you dress, how you participate in society – need to be affordable to have an acceptable living standard in the context of contemporary society.
- *Workers' surveys/voice.* Some campaigns (such as the Asia Floor Wage) have sought to involve workers in determining what is necessary for a living wage.

A very wide range of methods of calculating living wages draw on these three sources of information, commonly combining more than one of them, but with different approaches giving greater or lesser weight to different sources.

Agreement of lists of necessities by members of the public can create a "socially agreed" living standard which has a different meaning from a "scientifically" calculated standard determined by experts. Scientists may be good at specifying what nutrients are needed for adequate health, but less qualified to establish, say, what length of annual holiday, if any, should be considered part of a minimum acceptable standard of living in a given society at a point in time.

Calculations that are based on patterns of consumption or expenditure can take various forms. Some are based on observation of the things that people actually own or do: identifying "norms" by their prevalence. Others look at the amount spent on a particular category, say clothing, by people at a particular point in the income distribution (for example, if 80% of people spend at least $500 a year on clothes, it could be suggested that you need at least this amount to be able to dress like most people). This reference to actual expenditures can help avoid producing a requirement that is well out of line with how people actually live. However, to some extent consumption-based standards are circular. Imagine that a basic wage were designed to allow workers to finance a consumption level that 80 per cent of households exceed (that is, at the "20th percentile" of spending). If this system were applied in a country where existing inequalities prevented over 20 per cent of households from reaching a decent standard of living, then such a wage would help perpetuate inadequate living standards.

Another way in which spending patterns have been used is as a way of deducing the overall cost of living from scientific calculations of physical necessities. In the United States, the main poverty line is based on three times the cost of an economic food plan. This is based on the observation of households spending a third of their income on food. This observation was made in 1955, and incorporated into the current official poverty measure, adopted in the 1960s. Unfortunately, this method is massively outdated. This is partly because a food basket drawn up half a century ago bears little relationship to how people eat today, so merely uprating the items in the basket by inflation greatly understates what an adequate diet would now cost. This error is compounded by a factor of over two by the fact that food spending has become far smaller as a proportion of overall expenditure, so that in the United States today, an overall household budget is on average about seven rather than three times food expenditure (see Rosenheim 2015 for an insightful discussion of this).

This difference matters partly because many calculations of living wage rates in the US make use of the poverty line as a benchmark. In addition, some living wage calculations themselves infer spending requirements in some categories (such as leisure) with reference to how much people on modest incomes currently spend in these areas relative to others where material requirements can be measured scientifically, such as food (see Box 2.1). While such estimates do use contemporary rather than old evidence on spending patterns, they are very crude ways of estimating need. For example, if people on modest incomes spend on average half as much on leisure as on food, such an approach deduces that having an adequate

BOX 2.1 A MIXED APPROACH TO CALCULATING A LIVING WAGE IN THE UNITED STATES

Calculations of living wage levels in the United States generally draw on a wide range of data, combining scientific calculations of people's material needs with information on consumption patterns. Various nationally devised methods also allow living wages to be adjusted to local prices by local campaigns. One example is the Family Budget Calculator compiled by the Economic Policy Institute (2015), a Washington based thank tank. The components of household budgets comprise:

- Rent, based on "fair market rents", defined as rents at the 40th percentile in each metropolitan statistical area. Having enough to pay such a rent means that 40 per cent of homes suitable for your household size in your area would be affordable.
- Food, based on a scientifically calculated food plan, at a cost calculated nationally by the US Department of Agriculture. The calculation uses the second-cheapest of four plans, called a "low cost plan", allowing food meeting nutritional standards to be bought at a grocer and prepared at home.
- Child care, based on average costs, by state, for a suitable amount of child-care for children of various ages.
- Transport, based on vehicle miles travelled and the cost of owning and running a car. The number of miles is adapted for different settlement sizes, and based on surveys of how many miles are driven on average for purposes considered to be essential.
- Health care costs, based on paying premiums into a low cost plan, plus average out-of-pocket costs by region.
- Other costs – a wide category including other essential aspects of living such as household goods, clothing, entertainment, telephone services and personal care. This part of the calculation is based on how much people on low (but not very low) incomes actually spend on these categories, relative to housing and food. The income group considered is the "second fifth": those with incomes above the poorest 20 per cent of the population but below the best-off 60 per cent. These might be considered as people who are just getting by, and the amount they spend in these "other" categories is on average 48 per cent of what they spend on rent plus food combined. On this basis, the calculation assumes that to meet their needs, they have to spend 48 per cent as much on such categories as they would on a fair market rent plus a low cost food budget.

amount of leisure costs half as much as feeding yourself properly. Yet this deduction may be wrong: it is possible, for example, that meeting all leisure needs costs a similar amount to feeding yourself properly, but that people with limited incomes prioritize meeting their food rather than their leisure requirements. This makes it problematic to move from the scientific cost of an adequate diet to an estimate of meeting other needs, purely by observing how much people actually spend on different categories.

Which techniques are used to measure needs that go beyond physical survival may partly reflect the importance attached to the ability of a living wage to meet these wider requirements. In less affluent societies where relatively more of a family budget is spent on food and shelter, a fairly crude proxy of what it costs to meet wider needs may feel sufficient. For example, the Asia Floor Wage provides for a budget representing twice the cost of a food basket, assuming that food is by far the biggest component of the budget, even though the remainder is intended to include some provision for other items such as children's education and some leisure. In countries where food is only a small proportion of what people spend, on the other hand, the way that other needs are estimated acquires relatively greater importance.

In the United Kingdom, "consensually" derived household budgets – based on public agreement about what people need in each area of life – have emerged as the main basis for setting a living wage level. The first version of a living wage, applied to London, was based largely on a combination of an expert-based list of items that households need to buy (prepared by the Family Budget Unit in the late 1990s) and a relative poverty line. However, by the time this was extended nationally in 2011, new research was being regularly carried out that allowed the calculation of the accredited UK Living Wage to be linked to lists of items that the public consider necessary for a minimum living standard. This benchmark, the Minimum Income Standard for the United Kingdom (see Box 2.2), has the advantage of giving a living wage credibility in terms of public acceptance. On that basis, the Living Wage Commission set up in 2016 to establish a single calculation method for accrediting living wages across the country decided that the Minimum Income Standard should be the foundation of two living wage calculations, one for London and one for the rest of the country. In doing so, it emphasized that a living wage should "accurately reflect the views and experiences of people ... about what is required to

BOX 2.2 THE MINIMUM INCOME STANDARD: A SOCIALLY AGREED MINIMUM

The Minimum Income Standard is a method for researching what budget is required for a minimum acceptable standard of living, based on consensus among members of the general public. First developed by the universities of Loughborough and York in the United Kingdom in 2008, it has been copied by research teams in other countries including Ireland (where it is used as the basis of a living wage campaign), France and Japan, and in 2016 was piloted in the different contexts of Mexico and South Africa. In the United Kingdom, the research, funded by the Joseph Rowntree Foundation, is repeated regularly by the Centre for Research in Social Policy at Loughborough, to keep up with changes in contemporary society and in costs. Minimum budget requirements for a wide range of households are published annually, allowing the standard to be the cornerstone of living wage calculations.

The research involves groups of members of the public discussing in detail what would have to be included in the budgets of households with different compositions, in order to reach a minimum with the following definition (adapted by members of the public in each country where the research takes place):

> A minimum standard of living in the UK today includes, but is more than just, food, clothes and shelter. It is about having what you need in order to have the opportunities and choices necessary to participate in society.
> (Davis *et al*. 2015)

Through a sequence of groups tasked with agreeing lists of items that meet this definition, this process has identified a clear consensus over what distinguishes "need to have" from "nice to have" (but non-essential) items, based on clear rationales. A mobile phone is considered essential in modern Britain, because without it you could not participate socially at an acceptable level. A foreign holiday, while widely accessible, is not included in the minimum, because groups consider a week's holiday in the UK to be an adequate alternative in meeting minimum recreational needs. The groups are informed where needed by experts, for example over nutritional and heating requirements, but make the final decisions about what to include. Items are costed at national chain stores by the researchers and compiled into household budgets.

fully participate in society, and how social norms and needs change over time" (Living Wage Commission 2016: 5). In Canada, a different form of consensus-building involved four stages: a stakeholder/expert panel setting out criteria for a living wage; an expert calculation of what it cost to meet these criteria; consultation with focus groups of employers and people on low incomes responding to the results and their further revision by experts in light of these comments (Richards *et al.* 2008).

This explicit linking of public opinion with the living wage level is one way of influencing political credibility of a living wage: in the UK, it has allowed it to be presented as a socially agreed standard. Another aspect of the calculation that can influence the political meaning of a living wage is its linkage to a poverty line. Poverty is commonly used to describe an income at which it is considered that people are likely to suffer unacceptable hardship, and which therefore offends society's contemporary values. The idea that if you work you should not be in poverty thus has a powerful resonance. On the other hand, linking the living wage to poverty can also make it seem relatively unambitious, if it aims only to meet a relatively "minimalist" standard such as the US poverty line. This helps explain why some US calculations set a living wage at 50 per cent above the poverty line, and why the original calculation of the London Living Wage in the UK (operating from 2005 to 2015) added 15 per cent onto a calculation that was partly linked to a poverty threshold. Using the poverty line to inform a wage standard also reinforces the great political significance of how poverty itself is calculated (see Box 2.3).

Whatever the approach to measuring what people need to live on, those who set living wages know that there is no point specifying a level that seems unacceptably high to employers who adopt it or politicians who mandate it. "The mathematical computation of the living wage", writes one commentator, "is a political act" (Ciscel 2002: 51). This perhaps overstates things: a living wage without a consistent, credible calculation method has less chance of acquiring and maintaining authority with employers and the public, so campaigners and politicians cannot simply choose any figure they want. However, they will always seek a method that produces results within what are considered realistic bounds. In New Zealand, the research centre tasked with defining the level of income that families need "to live with dignity and to participate as active citizens in society", in order to set a living wage rate, attempted to incorporate public views through focus

BOX 2.3 DO POVERTY LINES SERVE AS ADEQUATE BENCHMARKS FOR WAGE STANDARDS?

Like living wages themselves, the poverty lines that can inform the calculation of a living wage can be calculated in many different ways. A useful distinction is between those that represent a more or less fixed living standard or set of goods and services and those designed to move in line with changing standards. As described above, the US poverty line fits into the first category: it is indexed to the cost of a basic diet. A crude indicator of extreme poverty used by the World Bank across countries is the number of people living on incomes below the equivalent of US$1.90 a day in local prices. In European countries, in contrast, poverty lines most commonly refer to a certain percentage of an average income – most commonly, to 60 per cent of the median. What this means is that you are considered to be in poverty if your income is worth at least 40 per cent less than that of the person in the middle of the income distribution. Such "relative income measures" are based on the idea, most famously formulated by the British sociologist Peter Townsend, that poverty changes with social context: households are in poverty if their "resources are so seriously below those commanded by the average family that they are in effect excluded from ordinary living patterns, customs, and activities" (Townsend 1979). A living wage referenced on a poverty line that changes with society has more chance of producing incomes considered adequate than one set at a constant level (even if adjusted by inflation).

Acknowledging that either a poverty line or a living wage should go beyond subsistence does not in itself mean that it will be considered adequate. The Indian constitution guarantees that "The State shall endeavour to secure, by suitable legislation or economic organization or in any other way ... a living wage, conditions of work ensuring a decent standard of life and full enjoyment of leisure and social and cultural opportunities". Originally interpreted mainly in terms of material essentials, assumptions underpinning the minimum wage included the cost of festivals and celebrations from 1991 onwards. The minimum wage is seen as an important tool for reducing poverty, and since 2005, there have been efforts by a series of commissions to redefine the poverty line in a way that includes costs such as education, health, electricity and transport, rather than just nutritional requirements. However, politically based differences among India's states about what proportion of the population should be considered to be in poverty have repeatedly prevented any single measure from being accepted (*Hindustan Times* 2016).

groups (King & Waldegrave 2012: 3). In the event, it concluded that these groups "produced estimates that were considerably higher than what might in the end be agreed as a defensible and achievable level" for the living wage (*ibid.*). As a consequence, the living wage was instead defined by an expert panel using data from various surveys on costs of food, housing, household costs, clothing, education, communications, health care and childcare. Yet such judgements about the realistic boundaries of living wage demands are not always straightforward. When the "fight for $15" campaign was first launched in the United States in 2012, it seemed utopian in calling for over double the federal minimum wage; within four years, several major cities and two states had agreed to adopt this level.

The size of household and working patterns

A single person working full-time requires a very different hourly wage rate to reach an adequate living standard than, say, a lone parent working part-time needs to provide for a family of three. Therefore, no one wage rate represents an adequate threshold for all households. Nor can employers be asked to pay people different amounts according to their family situation. A single living wage rate therefore serves as a compromise.

There are several ways in which this can be approached. One option is to set a living wage adequate to support a family of a particular size, on the basis that it is important for a typical family to have enough pay to support itself, which involves accepting that a single person may get guaranteed a wage considerably higher than the minimum required. Many living wages are calculated based on a single family type. The New Zealand and Canadian living wages, for example, are based on a family composed of two adults and two children.

The opposite view is that a living wage should be set at a baseline sufficient for a single person working full-time, and that measures other than a wage baseline, such as the payment of family benefits, are needed to secure adequate living standards for families. In Ireland, for example, a living wage used as a benchmark for campaigners is based on the needs of people without children. A compromise between these approaches, used in the United Kingdom, takes an average of wages required by a range of household types. In the United States, various budget/wages calculators (see Box 2.1 above) typically produce examples of earnings requirements for families of specified types in each area, allowing local living wage campaigners to make their own decisions about whether to use a single family type or an average.

A closely related issue is what assumption about working hours the calculations are based on. In general, they are worked out as if all adults in the household work full-time, and ask what hourly wage rate they would need in order to meet the required budget. Even though many households include adults not working full-time, such an assumption means that a living wage at least gives a household the opportunity of reaching the specified living standard, regardless of whether some may choose to trade income for leisure by working fewer hours. One alternative is to assume that it should not be necessary for all parents to work full-time to make ends meet, and that at least one parent in each household should be able to work part-time or not at all, in order to spend time looking after children. The calculation in New Zealand, for example, assumes one parent working full-time and the second working half time.

Assumptions about household types and working hours are more than just technical issues: like the method used to calculate needs, they affect what a living wage represents. Living wages assuming that one person in a couple should have to support a family are criticized by feminists as promoting a patriarchal model of provision. Conversely, if you assume that both parents must work full-time, this could be said to neglect work–life balance. Moreover, the size of family that a living wage is assumed to provide for interacts with expectations about how much the state should contribute to covering the cost of children, as discussed further in Chapter 4.

Figure 2.1 shows an example of how a calculation moves from the cost of an acceptable household living standard to the establishment of a living wage.

Adjusting living wages over time

Modern living wages have partly been a response to widening wage inequalities, and in some cases the deterioration in the value of minimum wages. The method of updating is therefore important. Many living wages are increased in line with prices. Most living wage ordinances in the United States have set a standard that is either relative to poverty thresholds or indexed to rise with the Consumer Price Index. For example, Madison, Wisconsin sets the living

	1. How much does a household need to live on (weekly?)		2. What hourly pay rate is needed to attain this, taking account of taxes and benefits?		3. Weighted according to representation of each household type in population		
					% of households		weighted wage
Single	£287.07	⟶	£8.85	x	32.5%	=	£2.88 +
Couple	£426.87	⟶	£6.00	x	33.7%	=	£2.02 +
Lone parent 1 child	£468.88	⟶	£12.83	x	5.1%	=	£0.65 +
Lone parent 2 children	£594.29	⟶	£16.32	x	2.6%	=	£0.42 +
Lone parent 3 children	£731.27	⟶	£18.40	x	1.1%	=	£0.20 +
Couple 1 child	£558.19	⟶	£7.56	x	10.8%	=	£0.82 +
Couple 2 children	£680.05	⟶	£9.32	x	10.3%	=	£0.96 +
Couple 3 children	£819.94	⟶	£11.69	x	2.9%	=	£0.34 +
Couple 4 children	£1040.46	⟶	£13.90	x	1.0%	=	£0.14
							= £8.43 weighted average, rounded to £8.45 for living wage

Figure 2.1 Moving from a minimum acceptable standard of living to a living wage: the UK calculation.

Based on all parents working full-time and paying for childcare for younger children. Figures for families with children are weighted averages for different age combinations.

Source: D'Arcy and Finch (2016)

wage for public employees and contractors at 110 per cent of the poverty line; the city of Chicago updates wages paid to city contractors each July according to the Consumer Price Index; and in Boston, the living wage for public contractors is adjusted every July, either to 100 per cent of the federal poverty level, to 110 per cent of the state or federal wage, or increased with the Consumer Price Index, whichever is the highest.

Price-based increases can be helpful in guaranteeing that a living wage will not fall in value over time as has happened for example with the US federal minimum wage. However, over a long period of economic growth and growing average wages, a price-based wage standard will deteriorate in relative terms, and potentially make low-paid workers less able to keep up with changing social norms. This indeed has been a difficulty with using a poverty line in the United States whose absolute value has not changed since the 1960s, despite the country having become far more affluent. One alternative is therefore to set increases in line with average earnings. Another is to continue to recalculate living wage requirements to ensure that they remain in line with contemporary needs. This is the approach taken in the United Kingdom and Ireland, based on recurring research on the Minimum Income Standard.

Yet continuous recalculation of what is needed to meet a wage adequate for a minimum standard can potentially throw up two related difficulties. One is that it can create irregular movements in the level of the living wage, that are problematic for employers who pay it. If new research showing that certain household needs and costs have increased coincides with a difficult economic period in which general wage increases are low, the increase in the wage bill may be hard for employers to afford. The risk of this happening could act as a serious disincentive for employers to sign up voluntarily for living wage accreditation.

The other problem is that a continuous recalculation could interact with other public policies affecting living standards in problematic ways. For example, at a time of fiscal austerity, a cut in cash benefits for working families would, on a recalculation of the wage needed, require employers to make up the difference in order to maintain minimum living standards. Chapter 4 shows that it is important to confront directly the respective roles of the state and employers in providing for low-income workers. Where there is no stable understanding about these respective roles, living wage employers may feel vulnerable to having to award sharp pay rises in tough economic times when they can least afford it.

One response to these risks has been to put a cap on how much the living wage is able to go up in any one year, while continuing to refer to a contemporary standard as a benchmark. In Ireland, limits are placed on whether the living wage can go up faster than earnings, and in the UK, the Living Wage Commission (2016: 8) reserves the right to phase in any sudden increases in the calculated rate. This again underlines the way in which contemporary formulations of living wages and their levels will always be subject to wider economic and political considerations. Living wages today are not utopian ideals but derive from pragmatic campaigns to persuade employers and governments to adopt them. Living wage campaigners have no interest in creating standards that are too demanding ever to be implemented.

How are living wages being advocated and implemented?

Contemporary campaigns for living wages have had a variety of objectives in terms of implementation. To understand the characteristics of living wage movements, the nature of these campaigns needs to be considered alongside their different objectives, and the extent to which they have achieved them.

At the heart of these distinctions is the fact that there are many forms that a "living wage" can take. In some cases it is simply a bargaining position – used for example by some US trade unions when negotiating with employers. More tangible agreements and regulations that may be referred to as "living wages" often take one of the following main forms:

- *A voluntary employer standard.* Employers agree to maintain wages at least at the living wage level advocated by campaigning groups and sometimes by an accrediting body.
- *A requirement of public contractors.* Typically, municipal governments agree statutory ordinances requiring anyone receiving public funds to pay at least a living wage.
- *A compulsory minimum for all employers.* Central or local governments set a minimum wage that is portrayed as a living wage, often because it is higher than a previous level.
- *A supply chain agreement.* Companies or groups of companies in an industry agree only to purchase from suppliers who pay workers receiving a living wage, and who themselves buy from such suppliers.

The nature of campaigns is influenced by which kind of living wage(s) they are seeking. This section looks at some characteristics of these campaigns, before considering how they have pursued each form of living wage.

New styles of coalition

While the contemporary US living wage movement dating from the 1990s has strong Christian origins, the influence of Christianity takes a radically different form than it did in the time of Catholic writers such as John Ryan a century earlier. The initial impetus came not from the writings of a Christian thinker, but from local church groups working at soup kitchens in

Baltimore, who were encountering increasing numbers of people unable to make ends meet despite having a job, often in low-paid services contracted by the city. Their specific solution to this, developed by working alongside the workers affected to formulate their own solutions, was to persuade the city government to pass an ordinance to require contractors to pay their workers a living wage. The longer-term impact was to inspire the growth of local coalitions seeking to combat low pay throughout the United States. These brought together a range of community groups, trade unions, think tanks and other campaigners (see for example Box 2.4).

One crucial departure of these pay campaigns from those prevailing for most of the twentieth century has been that they have not revolved around trade unions carrying out collective bargaining. Collective bargaining continues, but in parallel efforts to improve general wage floors, unions play a

---

BOX 2.4 COMMON CAUSE IN COMMON SPACES: LIVING WAGE AIRPORTS AND LIVING WAGE OLYMPICS

Living wage campaigns have been good at bringing together many types of campaigners to fight a common cause. One thing that can help create focus is where there are many low-paid service workers within a single well defined space – such as an airport or a large-scale sporting event.

Starting in the late 1990s, the Los Angeles Alliance for a New Economy, an advocacy organization for new economic approaches, drove a campaign to get all employers located at the three main Los Angeles airports to pay a living wage. This campaign also involved local community groups, trade unions through the American Federation of Labor and Congress of Industrial Organizations (AFL-CIO), an environmental health and justice organization called Communities for a Better Environment and the faith-based organization Clergy and Laity for Economic Justice. Joining forces helped these bodies to succeed in a large-scale unionization drive among those employed at the airports. This eventually led to the 1999 extension of a living wage covering city contracts to include businesses granted concessions to operate in airports – from cleaning firms to fast-food restaurants. The campaign was able to succeed by mobilizing people working alongside each other but for different employers, in airports as a common area over which the city government had the authority to impose such a wage ordinance (Bernstein 2004; Fairris *et al.* 2015; Luce 2005). This set precedent for subsequent living wage campaigns in other airports across the country, achieving higher wages for workers in major cities including New York, Washington DC, Seattle, San Francisco and Miami. Following on from the success of the airport campaigns, wider campaigns to increase city-wide or state-wide minimum wages have succeeded in producing a higher minimum for all employees in each of these cities.

London's 2012 Olympics, which claimed to be the first Living Wage Olympics, followed a different pathway. Even before the city's Olympic bid was won, Telco and London Citizens, community organizers in East London got involved in seeking to ensure that these games benefited the areas where they were held, an important factor for awarding the games. Through constant negotiation with various organizing bodies, they secured agreement in principle that workers for the many builders, retailers, cleaners and catering organizations involved in preparing and holding the games should at least be paid the London Living Wage. Although implementation was not perfect, the high profile of this event created an incentive for ethical behaviour by all the commercial organizations involved, and helped give a higher profile to workers doing the less glamourous jobs needed to make the Olympics a success. As with US airports, the application of a living wage to a defined geographical space, within which small companies generally needed a license to operate, helped counter the usually highly dispersed nature of low-paid service jobs, to create a powerful focus on setting a wage standard.

---

different role. Here, their influence comes not as representatives of specific workers in talks with their employers, but rather by making common cause with campaigners, putting public pressure on state authorities and employers to give the worst-paid workers a fair deal.

This pursuit of a general standard rather than just the particular interest of a group of workers has the potential to create tensions with some trade unions. Those whose members are not the least well paid may fear that if priority is given to raising wages at the bottom, their own members could lose out. Moreover, in the United States, where living wage ordinances often do not cover directly employed public workers, unions representing those workers sometimes fear that obliging contractors to pay higher wages will make contracting more expensive and leave less scope for raising public sector pay. Despite these tensions, unions have generally been supportive of living wage campaigns, and peak organizations such as the AFL-CIO in the United States and the Trade Union Congress in the United Kingdom have explicitly embraced the idea.

A crucial feature of a new union role in campaigning for wage floors is that it can address a central factor behind the decline of trade unions in developed countries in recent years. This is the decline in the manufacturing and directly employed public sector workforces, and the growth of service-sector workers, often poorly paid. Organizing such workers, who tend to be dispersed rather than in large workplaces, has been difficult. However, the experience of the Service Employees International Union, a prime organizer of the "Fight for $15" campaign in the United States, has shown the potential for bringing such workers into new campaigns. Starting with a wave of fast-food worker strikes in 2012, they have enjoyed widespread success in getting state and city governments to increase minimum wage rates sharply. The fact that such increases have often been put to citizens through the ballot box, and proved highly popular among voters, illustrates how pay improvement has become a public cause.

While the US experience of living wage campaigns has been copied in many respects in other countries, the nature of its organization has had significant differences as well as commonalities. The origins in the UK, starting in East London, drew direct inspiration from US experience, deriving from grass roots bodies and adopting community organizing techniques (Box 2.5). However, as the campaign spread nationally, extending from London Citizens to Citizens UK, its organizers sought to avoid what was perceived as an important weakness of the US campaign: its fragmentation, with multiple campaigns making different demands and setting different rates. This was particularly important in the UK context, where influencing a municipal government was less central than in the United States. In the UK, a national

THE FIGHT FOR $15

What is really significant about the Fight for $15 movement is – most labour disputes, look inside, they're about a group of workers covered by a collective bargaining agreement. In the Fight for $15, unions are helping to organize on a community basis, a group of workers who are on the fringe of the economy. It's not about union members protecting themselves. It's about moving other people up. This is the whole civil rights movement all over again.

Professor Gary Chaison, Clark University
(quoted in Greenhouse & Kasperkevic 2015)

BOX 2.5 COMMUNITY ORGANIZING: ADVOCACY WITH A DIFFERENCE

Political change is often achieved through political parties or advocacy groups acting on behalf of various interests within the community. In contrast, "community organizing" seeks to enable members of communities to come together to formulate and pursue their own agendas. In techniques pioneered by US activist Saul Alinsky and the Industrial Areas Foundation from the 1940s, community organizers aim to get alongside local people in deprived communities, listen to their concerns and help build leadership within these communities. The overall agenda is a radical one: the aim is for neighbourhoods to become places where people can meet to challenge forces that oppress them. They do so by bringing together previously isolated people to formulate specific demands and confronting those with power to change things.

The success of community organization in identifying low pay as a common cause and securing improvements for contractors in US cities has inspired similar campaigns in the UK. London Citizens is a community organizing group directly inspired by US techniques. In 2001, a group of parents in east London launched the Living Wage Campaign under the premise that existing wages did not allow them to "make ends meet". Faith groups, campaigners, businesses and community leaders joined this movement as a way of tackling working poverty. The swelling of living wage campaigns from small local beginnings to national mass movements shows this new kind of politics at its most successful.

---

perspective has been advantageous as campaigners have sought to get a living wage adopted by large companies operating throughout the country, and to influence policies to combat poverty that are largely designed nationally. Once the living wage became part of a national debate, it was greatly advantageous to establish a national accredited rate, adminstered by the UK-wide Living Wage Foundation, whose contrast with the legal minimum became a focus for debate. Two other countries, New Zealand and Ireland, created central bodies of this type from the start, and campaigns in Canada, while locally driven, are seeking to ensure a coordinated approach to encourage take-up by companies operating across jurisdictions.

One effect of living wage advocacy and negotiation, going beyond the context of worker representation, is that it offers potential for idealistic rather than self-interested coalitions. A good example of this is the activism of citizens in richer countries protesting about how globalization can create exploitation of workers in poorer ones. In common with movements such as Fair Trade, consumers can contribute to the rejection of products relying on exploited labour. The living wage perspective helps extend this from supporting the livelihoods of farmers by paying sufficient prices for commodities, to addressing wage rates used in producing manufactured goods.

The success of *voluntary employer standards* has perhaps been the most surprising outcome of living wage campaigns. In the United Kingdom, over 3,000 organizations, ranging from large retailers and manufacturers to public bodies such as the Scottish Government, many local authorities and public hospitals, to small start-up businesses, have registered as "living wage employers". In the United States, the movement has also acquired broader objectives, feeding campaigns for better state and federal minimum wages and also pressing large private employers and bodies such as universities to commit to paying a living wage. For example, the University of Virginia has implemented a rate of $11.76 an hour in 2016, well above the state minimum which remains equal to the federal rate $7.25. Other examples where university employees on the minimum wage earn higher wages than the federal and state minimum are Indiana University with $10.15 per hour, and Duke University, which has committed to gradually move from $12 to $15 by 2019.

The surprising aspect of this success is that, in tough economic times when both public and private bodies have often wrestled with tight budgets, they should be willing not just to raise wages but to commit to doing so in the future. Several factors may have contributed to this willingness.

First, some organizations today have a wage structure that more resembles an onion than a pyramid: only a relatively small number of workers (such as cleaners in an office-based organization) are doing the most menial, badly paid jobs. Some public bodies and large companies only have to increase wages of a small number of worse-paid workers by a relatively small amount to adhere to a living wage, and this therefore has a negligible effect on their pay bill. Other organizations have become "living wage employers" without having to raise anybody's pay. Some bodies have contracted out many of their worst paid service jobs, although if these are performed on site, contractors must pay the living wage as a condition for the host organization being accredited.

A second explanation is the importance of reputation to many bodies, which can have tangible effects on bottom lines. Large companies go to considerable efforts to develop a reputation as ethical traders that can affect business, and living wage campaigns have become part of that. A university that experiences vocal protests of students campaigning for a living wage for all staff may fear that a negative reputation could affect who chooses to study there. Importantly, once one or more organizations in a sector becomes a living wage employer, others fear that their reputations may suffer in comparison.

Third, as is discussed in Chapter 4, living wages can have positive effects on factors such as staff morale and retention. It is sometimes asked why, if decent pay reduces staff turnover and therefore brings a net financial benefit, employers need a campaign to encourage them to pay it. One potential answer is that seeing other employers following suit makes companies less likely to fear that they will be undercut in the short term, before these benefits materialize. Another is that staff loyalty is fostered not just by the level of pay itself but by the public expression of commitment by an employer announcing that it will pay a living wage.

Living wages that set *requirements on public contractors* potentially have wider and more systematic effects than voluntary sign-up by individual employers. Because they are ultimately funded by public money, there is potentially scope for the authorities who mandate these wages to ensure that enough funding is available to make living wages economical without job loss. However, when public authorities have their own resources severely limited by funding constraints beyond their control, there remains a big issue of how higher wages will be paid for. Indeed, one way of viewing the contracting out of public services is that it is partly motivated by an effort to get better "value for money" for taxpayers, but that this has only been achieved by the public sector turning its back on its role as an exemplar of paying decent wages in conventionally low-paid occupations. Requiring contractors to improve pay rates may help restore the public sector's role in promoting better pay for service providers, but ultimately this could require higher taxes.

There are important differences in the scope for mandating contractors to pay living wages in different countries. In the United Kingdom and European Union countries, competition laws have prohibited public bodies from making a given pay rate a direct condition for contractors bidding for work, although not from taking pay policies into consideration. Some UK local authorities who themselves have become living wage employers seek to favour suppliers who have also done so. In the United States, in contrast, city governments have started with requirements on contractors, and in only some cases have applied living wage mandates to their own workers.

A far more comprehensive adoption of a living wage occurs when a *compulsory minimum wage* is raised to a level described as a living wage. In 2015 the UK government announced that it would increase the minimum wage, then £6.50, to at least £9 an hour for workers over 25 by 2020, and call this the National Living Wage. This 38 per cent increase over five years would certainly not have happened without the pressure of voluntary living wage campaigns, even though a compulsory living wage had not been one of their demands. In the United States, increasing the minimum wage was one of the key ambitions for the Obama administration, but was blocked by Congress. Influenced by inaction at the federal level and by the growing strength of campaigns for a much higher minimum, in the twenty-first century states have become progressively bolder in setting their own rates, and cities have started to do so for the first time. After a number of mainly west-coast cities started to adopt the demand for a $15 rate, over twice the federal minimum, states also began to follow suit. In 2016, California and New York (for selective areas) committed to doing so by the early 2020s. The political language associated with these changes underlines the extent to which action on minimum wages has once again (as did Roosevelt when introducing the first federal minimum) borrowed the language of the living wage. Governor Gerry Brown, signing legislation to introduce a $15 minimum wage in California by 2022, made the following remarks:

> This is an old idea from the nineteenth century, from religious leaders: that work is not just an economic equation, but work is part of living in a moral community; a worker is worthy of his or her hire, and to be worthy means they can support a family. So economically, minimum wages may not make sense. But morally and socially and politically, they make every sense, because it binds the community together, and makes sure that parents can take care of their kids in a much more satisfactory way. That's the living family wage.
>
> (Quoted in Siders 2016)

Thus in the United States, what started with living wage ordinances for local government suppliers has also stimulated a far wider application of a higher minimum under the living wage banner. In some cases this creates several pay floors within a single state (Box 2.6).

Official adoption of a living wage into a compulsory minimum for all workers is, in one sense, the ultimate prize for living wage campaigns. The UK government estimated in 2015 that its higher minimum would eventually affect the pay of six million workers. This is of a different order of magnitude to the 150,000 workers whose pay the Living Wage Foundation estimated in 2017 had been affected by the voluntary rate, although this continues to grow and does not include indirect effects.

Despite welcoming such breadth of impact, campaigners also see risks in this official adoption. Their main fear is that a living wage label will be appropriated by public authorities who do not have a commitment to maintaining a wage at a genuinely adequate level. History confirms this risk: the living wage/minimum wage introduced by Roosevelt in the 1930s eventually declined in value and turned into a federal minimum widely regarded as a poverty wage. The United Kingdom's National Living Wage is not based on any calculation relating to living standards, although the intention of eventually pegging it to 60 per cent of average earnings would, if adhered to, be a powerful means of preventing the worst-paid workers falling behind.

BOX 2.6 SETTING WAGES IN MULTIPLE TIERS

The State of Maryland illustrates how successful implementation of a living wage at the local level has expanded to include both a minimum wage applicable to all workers that is higher than the federal rate, and an even higher living wage for state service contracts. In 1994, Baltimore was the first city in the country to pass a living wage ordinance, which was limited to public contracts. This was extended to contractors across the state in 2008. Two decades after Baltimore's implementation of the living wage, Maryland departed from its adherence to the federal minimum wage by setting an hourly rate $1 higher than the $7.25 national rate for all employees, scheduled to increase to $10.10 in 2018. As of 2016, the minimum wage in Maryland was $8.75; the living wage for Baltimore City contracts is $11.65; and the living wage for state contractors is $13.63 or $10.24 depending on the geographical area.

One criticism of the National Living Wage, discussed in Chapter 4, is that it was directly linked to cuts in working benefits, with the net effect of cutting rather than increasing family living standards.

So campaigners may mistrust the motives and consistency of governments purporting to incorporate the living wage idea into a compulsory minimum. One reason for them to do so is not related to the integrity of politicians but to the different characteristics of a statutory minimum. Where a wage floor is voluntary, it is hard for opponents to argue that adopting it will cause large numbers of job losses. Employers will adopt it as they feel able, and in doing so may strengthen their commitment to their employees, moving away from attitudes that see underpaid workers as expendable. An enforced wage rise across all sectors may, if too steep, cause some firms to shed labour. All things being equal, a voluntary living wage is likely to start harming employment (or have poor take-up because most employers find it unaffordable) at a higher level than a compulsory minimum. Moreover, the pressure for exemptions is likely to be greater in the case of a compulsory wage. One reason the UK government felt able to award a steep increase is because it excluded workers aged under 25, who are strongly represented in many low paid industries, and whose employment at lower rates could act as a safety valve for some employers feeling unable to pay the National Living Wage.

A final type of application of a living wage is through *supply chains*. Just as the absence of union protection and a less favourable pay structure in private compared to public organizations can create perverse incentives for public bodies to contract out labour, so large organizations with favourable pay terms can potentially cut costs by subcontracting to suppliers who protect their workers less well. This is an argument for responsible employers to make purchasing conditional on how their suppliers treat workers, including paying a living wage. Defining such an undertaking is not straightforward. Some decision has to be taken about which suppliers it applies to, and how far down a "chain". It seems there has to be some limit: does a large "living wage employer" require the caterer delivering sandwiches for its meetings to pay its employees a living wage? If so, what about the greengrocer who supplies the vegetables to the sandwich shop? And so on.

Nevertheless, the supply chain principle has been a particularly powerful means of bringing ethical pressure from consumers and consuming nations to address clear-cut exploitation of cheap manufacturing labour in developing countries, employed by suppliers to large multinationals who wish to be seen to trade responsibly. Agreements on standards among major brands can help avoid the risk that one country will undercut another by setting wages at excessively low levels. This requires clear-cut methods of setting wage standards across countries, such as through the Asia Floor Wage. Since the Rana Plaza complex collapse in 2013, Bangladesh, Cambodia, China, Indonesia, Malaysia, and Sri Lanka have either introduced or raised minimum wage rates; however they have been set to levels that campaigners say is still far too low. Wage rates in these countries need to be seen in the context of other aspects of working conditions. For instance, in Bangladesh, Cambodia, India and Malaysia minimum wage rates are based on a 48-hour working week, and some critics have said that higher wages without other labour regulations may be an attraction for girls who would prefer to go into the labour market and drop out of school (and who are more likely to do so at a young age than boys).

Commentary

Although the living wage represents a single core idea, that people should be paid enough to live at a reasonable level, we have seen that its interpretation and application varies across several dimensions. Its appropriate level can be related to perceptions of need as defined by experts or by the public, or alternatively use prevailing levels of income or consumption as reference points. It can seek to be sufficient to support a family, just a single worker or be based on an average of various cases. Campaigns may seek to persuade individual employers to pay living wages, have a wider reach through public contracting or supply chains or change the legal minimum for all workers to a level more adequate to live on. In general, living wage campaigns extend the quest for better pay beyond the direct representation of workers through trade unions, bringing together wider coalitions of advocates. Yet the characteristics of these coalitions vary greatly according to their origins and objectives. They can be focused at the community, national or global level.

At one level, this heterogeneity of living wage campaigns has the potential for being problematic. If "the living wage" means so many things in different contexts, it may eventually be seen as a dishonest term. An employer operating in two neighbouring towns, each with a campaign for a living wage, but set at completely different levels for no obvious reason, may find it hard to accept that it has a moral duty to pay it in both cases. In some countries there has been much greater geographical consistency, but waters are easily muddied when more than one version of a "living wage" comes into being, as has happened recently in the United Kingdom with the government version competing with the longer-standing, voluntary accredited living wage.

Yet looked at another way, the fact that there is no settled definition of the level or status of a living wage is actually an essential feature of its character. As discussed at the end of Chapter 1, a minimum wage can be precisely defined as a legal requirement, and the question "does country X have a minimum wage?" has a clear answer. Securing living wages, on the other hand, will always be a dynamic process, developing as society changes along with its norms and values. This applies not only to ensuring that a living wage relates to a living standard that is adequate for contemporary times, but also to its status and the interaction with policy goals and employment trends. For example, how far a living wage needs to provide for families of different sizes interacts with the level of family benefits, as discussed further in Chapter 4. The focus of living wages will always be influenced by where it is perceived that workers are being exploited – whether in sweatshops of Victorian England or present-day Asia, in the supply of public services through non-unionized contractors or in private service industries such as fast food, achieving low consumer prices only by setting low pay norms. In these varying contexts, the implementation of a living wage is not something that can be settled once and for all, but rather involves a continuous conversation about society's values: what is considered a decent living standard, where markets are falling short and what can be done about it.

Part of this conversation is about the extent to which it is appropriate to intervene in labour markets. Competing economic perspectives emphasize on the one hand the importance of letting the market for labour operate freely, and on the other, intervening to prevent the unequal distribution of power in these markets causing people to live on unacceptably low wages. This is the subject of the next chapter.

3

The impact of higher wage floors on labour markets

The exchange of a person's labour for a wage is a voluntary transaction between a worker and an employer at an agreed price. If the price is artificially set at a higher wage rate than the employer is willing to pay, the employee will not be hired. This simple truth causes some free market economists to argue against any "wage floor" (a minimum or living wage) that seeks to adjust wages according to any criterion other than the free operation of the labour market. To do so risks destroying jobs.

While that is the conclusion of neoclassical economic theory (on which prevailing modern economic models are based), many economists have suggested that in practice, the world is not that simple. The way that wages are actually fixed only imperfectly reflects what firms could pay for labour and still make a profit. The bargaining power of workers and employers is unequal. In some cases the ability of workers to move to higher-paying jobs if their work is undervalued (as market theory would predict) is restricted, sometimes because their firm is the only one hiring for a particular job type in a local area. Moreover, even if as the theory predicts, a rise in wages causes a fall in employment levels, the size of these effects needs to be taken into consideration. In 2015, the UK government announced a large increase in the minimum wage for over-25-year-olds by 2020. It estimated that this would eventually result in pay rises for six million workers, but reduce jobs growth by 60,000 (Office for Budget Responsibility 2015: 204). If that proves true, for every hundred people whose pay increases, one job (which does not yet exist, but theoretically would have by 2020) will not be created. Many people might think this is a reasonable way of improving workers' lives overall, rather than insisting that no pay increase can ever be worthwhile if it means fewer jobs.

This chapter considers the effect of wage floors on the labour market. "Wage floor" is here taken to mean any minimum pay rate that is agreed or enforced outside the context of market bargaining. Evidence of the effect of wage floors is most clear-cut where a minimum wage is imposed by law, and much of the evidence relates to minimum wages set as statutory requirements within particular countries or regions. A living wage adopted voluntarily by employers on the basis that it is right to pay enough for people to live on can also be regarded as a wage floor that overrides market bargaining. However, its impact can be harder to measure, partly because the decision by employers about whether to adopt a voluntary living wage is bound to be influenced by whether they think it is affordable. Nevertheless, those putting pressure on employers or governments to put any kind of "artificial" floor on wages need to consider the overall potential impact on the labour market of not allowing the market wage to prevail. This explains why much of this chapter looks at evidence on minimum wages rather than living wages, yet why such evidence is crucial for the subject of this book. Indeed, it could be argued that current efforts in the United States (from where much of this evidence derives) to restore minimum wages to more adequate levels after years of decline in their value represents a revival of Franklin D. Roosevelt's mission to make a minimum wage a living wage.

The chapter starts by summarizing theoretical arguments and counter-arguments about the potential adverse effect of wage floors on labour markets. It then considers what recent evidence has shown about, firstly, the effect on employment, and next on wider effects on employer and employee behaviour. The chapter concludes by reflecting on which consequences of setting wage floors are considered acceptable and unacceptable, by whom and why.

Free markets and market imperfections: economic arguments against and for minimum wages

The textbook model of supply and demand

Neoclassical economics suggests that as long as markets are allowed to operate freely, resources will be deployed most efficiently through the interaction of supply and demand to determine market prices. In the case of labour, Figures 3.1–3.4 present the basic textbook model, showing what happens if an enforced wage floor overrides the negotiated market price.

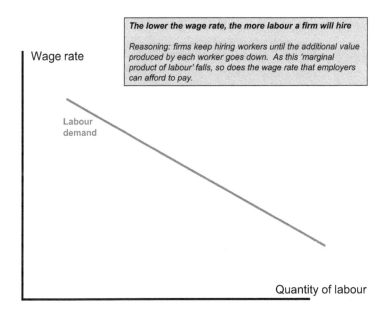

Figure 3.1 Labour demand.

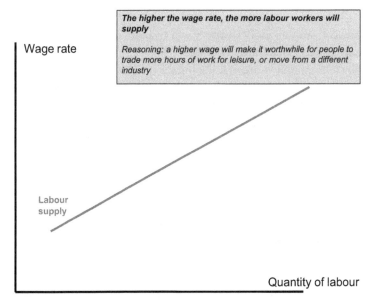

Figure 3.2 Labour supply.

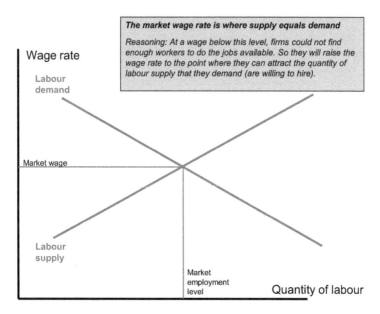

Figure 3.3 The supply–demand equilibrium.

In the basic economic model, buyers will usually "demand" (be willing to purchase) more of something the lower the price they can get it at; conversely, sellers will supply more of it the higher the price they can sell it for. These opposite relationships will produce an "equilibrium price" at which the demand and supply lines intersect: buyers are willing to purchase the same amount as suppliers wish to sell. This is also described as the "market clearing" price, since everybody wishing to buy or sell at this price can do so.

In the case of labour markets, if wages are initially lower than the market rate shown in Figure 3.3, some buyers/employers will be short of labour and be willing to bid the price up in order to secure workers from their competitors. If wages are too high, fewer jobs will be made available than workers want, so some will be willing to accept work at a lower wage, rather than be unemployed, and so bid down wages. Adjustments of this type occur until the equilibrium is reached.

A minimum wage set above the equilibrium, as in Figure 3.4, will reduce employment and prevent some people willing to work at this rate from

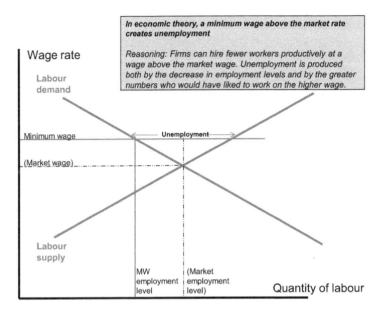

Figure 3.4 The theoretical effect of a minimum wage.

finding a job, causing unemployment. This will be the result of firms investing less in creating the jobs shown here, and redeploying capital for other purposes. While sometimes this can mean investing in more productive jobs (see below), making labour more expensive can also incentivize a switch in investment towards more "capital intensive" forms of production, meaning that it becomes relatively more economical for firms to invest in machinery and equipment rather than in workers to enhance output.

A central concept in the model explaining market wages is the *marginal product of labour*. This refers to the additional output that a firm can gain from hiring an additional worker. This helps determine labour demand and therefore the wage a firm is willing to pay. It is assumed that production is increased to a point where the marginal product of labour diminishes (because production capacity is stretched, so each additional worker adds less), producing the downward slope in labour demand shown in Figure 3.1.

Limitations in the textbook model

Economists recognize that the above model is a great oversimplification of how labour markets actually work. Importantly, it looks at a single industry in isolation and imagines labour to be homogeneous (such as where unskilled hands are needed to work machines in a factory). This means for example that it takes no account of the *quality* of labour, or the scope for raising productivity to fund higher wages, whether by investing in better equipment or in worker skills. Economic literature recognizes a great number of complexities in labour markets in practice, and it requires a study of labour economics to start to appreciate the many interactions involved. Here, it is sufficient to note six key factors that could influence the relationship between wages and employment, other than those shown in the model illustrated in Figures 3.1–3.4:

1 Even taking the model as accurate, the *sensitivity of employment rates to wages* can vary greatly. This depends in particular on the slope of the labour demand line shown in the diagram: if it is steep, the difference between the minimum wage employment level and the market employment level shown in the final panel will be small. A steeply sloping labour demand line means that relatively few additional jobs can be created by lowering wages by a given amount, suggesting that the marginal product of labour falls rapidly above a certain level of employment. This could occur for example if an additional worker is hired in a factory where machines are already being used to the maximum, or if an additional nurse is taken on in a hospital unit where a shortage of expensive medical equipment is causing a bottleneck in throughputs. Economists refer to this as low *price elasticity of demand* in labour markets, meaning that the quantity of labour that firms are willing to hire is relatively insensitive ("inelastic") to wage rates. The level of this elasticity has therefore been a focus of studies on the effects of minimum wages.

2 In practice, labour markets have many "imperfections", that do not fit the model. In particular, there is *imperfect competition* between employers. Under "perfect" market competition, an employer cannot pay a worker less than the marginal product of their labour (how much they add to output), because another employer would offer

them a higher wage. In reality, competition is constrained by the fact that workers cannot always readily switch employers.

One important reason for this is that there may not be another employer buying the same kind of labour close to where people live. This is referred to by economists as *monopsony*: just as a monopoly is where a market is dominated by a single seller, a monopsony refers to a single buyer – in this case of labour. A worker during the industrial revolution employed by the town's only cotton mill had little or no choice of working elsewhere, so their employer could set a wage below the rate that would have existed under market competition. In this case an enforced higher wage might not require the employer to cut back on jobs to ensure that workers produced the value of their wage, since previously they were producing more on average than it cost the employer to hire them and still make a profit.

Indeed, economic theory predicts that the result of forcing a monopsonistic employer to pay higher wages will be to *increase* employment, as long as wages are still no higher than they would have been in competitive conditions. This is because the higher wages will attract additional workers to accept jobs, allowing the firm to expand the numbers it employs without raising its average labour costs further.

3 In practice, *interactions between wage rates, productivity and labour costs* may strongly influence the long-term impact of setting wage floors. The simple model assumes that the marginal product of labour is fixed for a given quantity of labour (an additional worker is of a set value to the firm), and that higher wage rates will feed directly into higher labour costs. Neither of these things is necessarily true. An employer obliged to pay a higher wage may look for new ways of making workers more productive, for example by introducing new working practices or increasing training. Long-term labour costs may also be influenced indirectly by wage rates, for example if better paid workers leave their jobs less often and thus reduce the costs of recruitment and induction training. In industries with high turnover, this can have an important effect on costs.

4 Other *responses by employers* to increased labour costs resulting from a wage floor may be more varied and complex than adjusting employment levels to compensate for the higher wage. These may include passing on the additional cost in higher prices (which is more feasible

if all one's competitors also face the higher cost of a compulsory minimum wage, making them unable to maintain the original price) and reducing working hours but not the number of jobs. As discussed later, while the latter response is similar to cutting jobs in terms of reducing labour supply, it may be seen as less socially counterproductive than increasing wages for some workers only to make others unemployed. If the same low-paid workers have to put in fewer hours for a similar total pay packet, this could be seen as socially beneficial, although in such a case the question arises of whether that total truly produces a "living wage", if overall remuneration has not increased.

5   There are strong possibilities of *substitution* of one kind of labour for another as a result of a minimum wage being imposed, so that overall employment might not change. This may, for example, take the form of more skilled jobs being created to replace unskilled ones, as firms redirect investment into jobs that can support the higher wage. It can also potentially cause substitution by age if, as in some cases, there are different minimum wage rates for different age-groups. However, a nineteenth-century objection to minimum wages, which held that there is only a given pot of money available to pay all workers' wages ("wage fund theory") has been discredited. It is now recognized that the amount of wealth that can be allocated to pay is variable, even in the short term, and influenced by labour supply and demand.

6   Over the economy as a whole, *increased consumption* by workers who have had a pay increase can stimulate demand, and therefore improve the quantity of goods that firms can sell at a given price, allowing them to expand production. People on low incomes tend to spend rather than save a high proportion of their income, so this feedback of higher pay into increased economic activity is stronger in low-paying labour markets. The effect, however, is not easy to demonstrate, because the separate effect of a minimum wage is hard to distinguish from other influences on aggregate demand. It might be seen as one factor that helps explain why the overall measurable effect on employment is not as predicted in the model, but it would generally be hard to show that this factor fully cancels out negative effects on labour demand.

It is important to interpret such factors as showing that relationships between wages and employment levels can in practice be more complex than simple economic laws suggest, but not to pretend that these laws are irrelevant. Evidence presented below suggests that the predicted relationship is at best weak in practice, and that in many cases there is no discernible effect of wage floors on employment levels. However, this may be because such floors have been cautiously applied, to a degree or in circumstances unlikely to cause large worker lay-offs. The laws of supply and demand remain pertinent, in warning that at some level of enforced higher wages, employers will have no choice but to hire fewer people, or at the very least to reduce opportunities for people with lower skills or less experience. Those pursuing a living wage for all employees cannot completely ignore such a risk.

Wage floors and the labour market: the evidence

A large number of studies have sought in recent decades to measure the effects of minimum wages on labour markets and firms' behaviour. Initially, the emphasis of most economic research on this subject was designed to measure the strength of the effects predicted by the theoretical model, and in particular how serious was the predicted reduction in employment. From the 1990s, however, the studies started to be increasingly empirical rather than theoretical. That is to say, they no longer started from the assumption that the theory was correct, and where evidence did not match its predictions, sought to build alternative models of how the labour market actually works in practice. While this has not resulted in any single clear-cut understanding of how labour markets function, it has had two important consequences. The first is to make it clear, based on a mountain of evidence, that minimum wages do not systematically reduce employment levels. The second is to show, in selective ways, some different effects that they have, such as on prices, wage structures and staff turnover rates (see Card & Krueger 2016: ix–xxii for a concise summary of this history).

There is no clear-cut evidence overall that minimum wages reduce the number of jobs, and any observed effects tend to be small

Research can, broadly, seek to identify the effect of minimum wage laws on employment levels in three ways (Dolado *et al.* 1996: 330–32). One is to consider "before and after" effects of a minimum wage law or change in rate.

Interpreting this evidence can be difficult because other conditions affecting employment may vary over time, and some of these changes may affect the relationship between wages and employment. For example, a period of strong economic growth may encourage governments to raise minimum wages, but then it becomes difficult to compare the new employment rate to what it would have been in these improved economic conditions had the minimum wage not been raised.

The second way is to look at the structure of wages at any one time, in a country with a minimum wage, and to draw conclusions about the extent to which this statutory minimum skews the wage distribution. This however requires adopting a model that makes assumptions, which are difficult to verify, about what would be the structure of wages without an enforced minimum.

A third approach is to look at "natural experiments", in which there exist at one time two parallel situations that are similar in every respect except the level of the minimum wage. This potentially avoids the weaknesses of the other two approaches of not being able to control adequately for factors other than wage rates that could influence employment levels. Much attention has been given to such natural experiments in the form of neighbouring jurisdictions in the United States where minimum wage rates differ but other conditions are largely similar.

Research in the 1970s and 1980s on impacts of minimum wages in the United States and Europe tended to take the first two approaches, with inconclusive results. In European countries such as France and the Netherlands, the fact that minimum wages were higher as a percentage of earnings than in the United States was seen as helping to explain higher youth unemployment in Europe in those decades, which persists today. However, the minimum wage effect was not clearly demonstrated. It was hard to distinguish this effect from that of other forms of employment protection which could have influenced the hiring of young workers. Moreover, the European countries, unlike the United States, applied lower minimum wages for younger workers, reducing the potential for damage to youth employment (Dolado *et al.* 1996).

Research within the United States published in this period appeared initially to show that, as the minimum wage rate fluctuated relative to general wages, teenage employment was higher in periods when the minimum wage was lower – by about a tenth to a third of the proportion of the wages difference (see Box 3.1). However, the experience of the 1980s seemed to contradict this finding. The federal minimum wage was frozen from 1981 to 1990 and therefore fell by over a quarter in real terms due to inflation (see Figure 1.1, page 14). This appeared to have no stimulating effect on youth employment, as would have been predicted.

Ironically, the same decline in the value of the US federal minimum that seemed to contradict the theory that lower pay should increase employment also helped create better conditions for testing this theory. By the early 1990s, a number of states were trying to compensate for lower federal rates by setting their own minimum wages. This created the "natural laboratories" of businesses in neighbouring states having to pay different wage rates under economic conditions that in other respects were very similar. The most famous, landmark study looked at wages and employment in parts of New Jersey, which had increased its minimum wage, compared to neighbouring parts of Pennsylvania (an adjacent state), which had not (see Box 3.2). The results seemed to show that there was no discernible effect on employment (Card & Krueger 2016). This was followed by many similar studies of neighbouring counties in different states, that reached a similar conclusion. The most extensive research of natural experiments moved from a case study approach to a generalized comparison, by comparing every pair of adjacent counties over a state border with available data (316 pairs), over a lengthy period, 1990 to 2006. This study (Dube *et al.* 2010) again found no adverse employment effects.

BOX 3.1 WHEN HIGHER MINIMUM WAGES SEEM TO CAUSE LOWER EMPLOYMENT, HOW DO WE DESCRIBE THE SIZE OF THIS EFFECT?

US studies published in the 1970s and the 1980s appeared to show a negative relationship between minimum wage rates and teenage employment. The sensitivity of employment to wages was described as having an "elasticity" of between −0.1 and −0.3. This means that each 1 per cent increase in a minimum wage creates a decrease of employment of between 0.1 and 0.3 per cent. For example, if a minimum wage rose from $10 to $11 an hour (by 10%), a firm hiring 1,000 workers would on average reduce employment by between 10 and 30 workers (1–3%).

BOX 3.2 WHAT HAPPENED WHEN FAST-FOOD WORKERS GOT A PAY RISE IN NEW JERSEY, BUT NOT ROUND THE CORNER IN PENNSYLVANIA?

In 1992, New Jersey increased the minimum wage to $5.05, while the rate in neighbouring Pennsylvania remained at the federal level of $4.25 per hour. This provided a basis for research that is much closer to a clinical experiment than is normally possible in the real world. Using the terminology of experiments based on medical or other interventions, the areas where the wage was changed can be referred to as the *treatment group*, while those keeping the original wage are considered as a *control group*, in evaluating the impact of increasing wages.

The easiest way to test this was in a large and relatively standardized part of the US labour market: workers in fast-food restaurants. Economists David Card and Alan Krueger surveyed 410 fast-food restaurants in the neighbouring states, focusing on the impact on employment rates (Card & Krueger 1994). Their much quoted study found that far from costing jobs, a higher minimum wage actually had a positive effect on employment in the fast-food industry. New Jersey outlets that did not have to raise pay because they were already paying above the new minimum wage had the same employment growth as outlets in Pennsylvania, while those that had to increase their wages increased their employment rates.

The authors suggest various possible explanations for this result that went against received economic theory. The fact that fast-food restaurants exert considerable power in the labour market suggests that low minimum wages allow them to employ people at less than what they are worth, and enforced higher wages are not only affordable but draw more people into the job market, allowing the industry to expand. In addition, the higher minimum seems to have fed through into price increases. However, it could not have done so very directly, since price rises were similar where wages had been lower, and therefore were more affected by the increased minimum, as in restaurants where they had started off higher. Yet price rises affect different products within each restaurant differently: French fries seemed to fall in price and meals to increase, perhaps indicating some marketing strategy of attracting customers in, but still recovering the higher wage costs.

The reality is that economists can offer all sorts of hypotheses about how firms behave, but not confident explanations. This is because company behaviour is so often too complex, taking many factors into account, to be readily explainable through a simple economic model with a limited number of variables. As is so often the case: economists theorize; stuff happens. This stuff, which is external to the economic models, is referred to by economists as "noise", and often drowns out the effects they seek to identify.

It is nevertheless important that the central finding that higher wages did not cost jobs has been confirmed by many other studies throughout the United States. Yet this conclusion has not gone unchallenged. Neumark and Wascher (1995, 2000) concluded that in fact the higher minimum wage was associated with a 5 per cent fall in employment in the fast-food industry in New Jersey, but the authors of the original study, Card and Krueger (1998, 2000), carried out a further study confirming their findings, and pointing to flaws in Neumark and Wascher's work. As so often with competing academic teams, technical disputes about research design can be very hard to resolve. In this case they revolve around the ways in which pay is measured, with Neumark and Wascher saying they had a more reliable series of payroll data over time, while Card and Krueger claimed that this was flawed because Neumark and Wascher's findings could be explained purely by how results were affected by different intervals in reporting pay.

What happened next?

Research challenging the "minimum wages cost jobs" narrative has had an important effect overall on recent calls for higher minimum wages in the United States, but has not always noticeably affected policies in the states being studied.

Pennsylvania continued to stick to the federal minimum wage rate until 2016, when an increase of nearly $3 an hour was approved for state workers and state contractors in the janitorial, landscaping, delivery and food preparation services.

New Jersey continued to maintain hourly rates somewhat above the federal minimum between 1992 and 1997, then 2006 to 2009 and since 2010, but in intervening periods stuck to the federal rate. Interestingly, a new "natural laboratory" in the region is emerging – but a reverse of the original situation where the higher-wage scenario was tested in New Jersey. In 2016, New York passed legislation to increase the minimum wage towards $15 an hour, while New Jersey's governor Chris Christie vetoed a bill to do so, sticking with the much lower $8.38 an hour, rising only with the consumer prices index. These two neighbouring states are set to have wages much further apart than New Jersey and Pennsylvania 25 years ago. This could create dream jobs for labour market researchers, if not for New Jersey burger-flippers.

Such results do not mean that the debate about job losses has been resolved. Some economists, such as David Neumark, have argued that the evidence is far from conclusive, since some studies do show negative effects (Neumark & Wascher 2008). Many reviews of the evidence, however, have made the point that once you take account of differences in the reliability of results, the evidence shows no systematic effect on jobs (Schmitt 2013 reaches this conclusion in a review of "meta-studies" which themselves each round up the evidence). One aspect of this is the potential for results to be affected by background factors that have not been fully corrected for. An example is that some studies have found that regions with low minimum wages have tended to see high employment growth, without taking account of other characteristics of these regions. In particular, the American South has seen relatively strong economic growth, and is also generally conservative politically, electing state governments that are less inclined to raise minimum wages than elsewhere. This does not however mean that the lower wages explain the growth, to which many factors have contributed (Dube *et al.* 2010).

A further important aspect of the US evidence is that impacts, where identified, tend to be small. Figure 3.5 shows the size of effect of various studies. Three particular results stand out. First, for most studies there is only a minor effect. Second, where the effect is somewhat larger, it is as likely to be positive as negative (a higher minimum wage associated with more rather than fewer jobs). And third (not shown directly on the graph), there is a bias for more reliable or precise studies to give smaller estimates. The overall median elasticity is –0.05, but the "precision-weighted" median (giving more weight to more reliable results) is just –0.03. This is only a tenth to a third of the effects estimated in the 1970s and 1980s mentioned earlier in this chapter. That is to say, an increase in a minimum wage from $10 to $11 (by 10%) is associated with a fall in employment in a 1,000-worker firm of just three employees (0.3 per cent). Given the degree of variability of study results and hence imprecision in estimating the exact level of the relationship, this overall result can be considered negligible.

Outside the United States, the most extensive and systematic research on the impact of a minimum wage has been carried out in the United Kingdom. The Low Pay Commission, which sets minimum wage rates, has a brief to warn against any evidence of wages harming job prospects, and commissions research to evaluate this (e.g. see Low Pay Commission 2016). Unlike

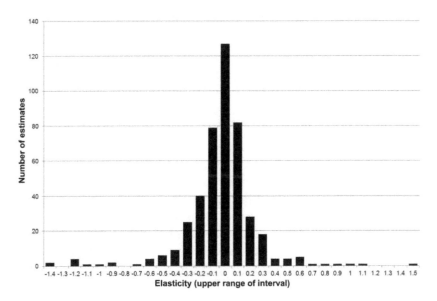

Figure 3.5 Sensitivity of employment and hours to changes in minimum wage: results of 439 US estimates.

This chart summarizes the results of over 400 calculations within 23 different studies showing the "elasticity" of employment in response to wage changes in different ranges. For example, the greatest number of studies (shown by the highest bar) put the figure at between zero and −0.1 (i.e. a 1 per cent increase in pay will reduce employment by up to 1 out of every 1,000 workers). Positive results show that higher minimum wages are associated with more rather than fewer jobs.

Source: Belman & Wolfson (2014); data kindly supplied by authors

in the United States, the UK does not offer "natural experiments" comparing neighbouring areas at a point in time, since the minimum wage is national. Rather, the research has closely scrutinized differences between employees and sectors affected and unaffected by minimum wage increases. As summarized by a thorough review of such evidence by Metcalf (2008), here too it was found that there has been little or no impact on employment.

The context of the UK research is significant. It is part of a process whereby a cautious policy of raising the minimum wage only to the extent that it does not harm jobs is supported by a system that gives a warning signal if such harm is detected. So far this warning has not been triggered. On the one hand, this creates confidence that the minimum wage is beneficial. Were it to be raised to a rate that reduced employment, this could damage the reputation of the minimum wage, even if the harm were relatively minor and if suitable adjustments were then made. On the other hand, by never testing it to that level, it is uncertain whether the process has been overcautious.

This dynamic may now change. In announcing a large, politically determined increase in the minimum wage for over-25s between 2016 and 2020, and asking the Low Pay Commission to advise on progress towards this level but not on the level itself, the UK government has dropped its former caution. This will be testing the sensitivity of employment to a minimum set at levels not previously tried. The government has predicted a near-negligible effect on jobs – a 38 per cent increase over five years causing a reduction of only 60,000, or about 0.2 per cent of the total number of jobs. However, this is based on a theoretical model of labour demand which cannot be checked directly against reality, since the conditions that it measures have not previously existed. As described in Chapter 2, a number of US cities and states are also breaking new ground in terms of the rate at which the minimum wage is being lifted, by phasing in a rate of $15 an hour, over twice the present (2016) federal minimum. All of these cases have been inspired by living wage campaigns, and thus given comparatively greater weight to moral than to economic arguments. The research showing that fears of economic harm have so far not been realized clearly encourages legislators to be bolder in pursuing wages considered to be adequate in covering living costs. Whether this boldness is merited will be tested by future research on economic impacts.

The possibility of substitution of jobs, especially across age groups, must be taken seriously

It is important to distinguish between the effect of minimum wages on *overall employment rates* and the *employment chances of individual groups*. In particular, if groups with low wages also have low productivity, efforts to help them by setting a minimum wage will be counterproductive if the result is that firms hire a different set of workers better equipped to produce more. If firms seek to raise production by employing workers with higher skill levels, substitution of less-skilled with better-skilled workers is one possibility, although another, more benign outcome is for employers to train existing workers to become more productive. On the other hand, insofar as productivity is linked to age and experience rather than skills that can be readily acquired through training, displacement of younger, less experienced workers may be the only option.

Many of the studies already referred to focus on employment outcomes for younger workers, since they tend to be the worst paid and the earliest affected by a statutory minimum – especially in the United States where minimum wages do not tend to discriminate by age. The relatively low level of US minimum wages, even in relation to teenagers' productivity, helps explain why their employment rates have not been clearly affected. Previous studies showing some effect on teenage employment in the 1970s (when the US minimum was considerably higher) did not identify any compensating effect on adult employment. But in Europe, where adult minimum wages tend to be much higher relative to average pay, the placing of age boundaries and how much below the adult rate the youth rate is set can be key issues (see Box 3.3).

An important argument for setting younger adults' wages at a lower rate is that they need a chance to acquire skills, by being paid less at a time when they are relatively less productive. If employers are deterred from hiring them on this basis, it is argued, they will lose out by never getting a chance to acquire these skills. The centuries-old practice of apprenticeship involves workers spending a period on very low wages while they are being trained. This practice can also be related to the issue of a living wage: many young adults have lower living costs, for example because they are not yet raising a family. Historically, apprentices often lived with their employers in very simple conditions. Yet both the accuracy and the ethics of this assumption can be criticized. Some people start a family at age 18, others at 40, so age-based pay rates will not accurately reflect the different costs that people face. And on a point of principle, an attempt to vary pay with living costs is problematic. People working side by side do not get paid different amounts according to the size of their families, so why should they purely on the basis of chronological age? This explains why, for example, the living wage rate accredited by the UK's Living Wage Foundation uses a single calculation for all workers.

Age-discriminating minimum wages may nevertheless be seen to be realistic in terms of preventing jobs from being lost by workers at an age where on average they are relatively unproductive. A projection of what

BOX 3.3 DO YOUNG EUROPEANS GET PRICED OUT OF WORK?

In comparison to the UK and the United States, many continental European countries are often characterized as having relatively "inflexible" labour markets, in which rules about hiring people, payroll taxes and relatively high minimum wages deter employment. This is particularly relevant for young workers whose lack of experience makes them comparatively less productive, and could help explain high rates of youth unemployment seen in some European countries, which in some cases rose above 50 per cent in the wake of the 2007/8 financial crash.

An underlying difficulty in identifying the role of minimum wages in contributing to this phenomenon is that their influence is hard to distinguish from other, highly distinctive features of employment conditions in each country. Many European countries have complex employment regulation, and apply it in different ways to different groups of workers. Even when considering the price of hiring people, minimum wages need to be looked at in combination with "social charges": the payroll taxes imposed on firms to help fund social security and other programmes, which can make the total cost of hiring someone considerably greater than their pay. One study found for example that while the United Kingdom and Spain set minimum wages at an identical percentage of average wages, employers had to pay an additional 31 per cent in payroll taxes or social insurance contributions in Spain but only 7 per cent in the UK for a full-time minimum wage worker (in 2005: see Immervoll 2007).

One thing that is clear is that there is huge variation in different European countries. Figure 3.6 compares their minimum wage and youth unemployment rates. It shows that German-speaking and Nordic countries, which have not used general minimum wages but rather tailored wage regulations to different industries and occupations, have succeeded in keeping youth unemployment extremely low. Germany is often compared to France (for example by Cahuc *et al.* 2013) in these terms, with the suggestion that France's high minimum wage rates explain why its youth unemployment is so much higher than Germany's. However, the graph shows that Italy has no minimum wage but higher youth unemployment than France, while countries like Greece and Spain have much higher youth unemployment than others such as the United Kingdom and Luxembourg, despite minimum wages being at similar levels (relative to median wages in each country). This does not mean the level of the minimum is irrelevant, and in some cases specific design features may contribute to these results. Luxembourg and the UK both have lower

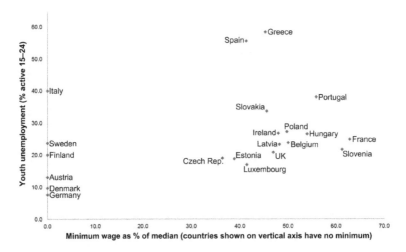

Figure 3.6 Minimum wages and youth unemployment rates in 21 European countries, 2013.

Sources: OECD; Eurostat

minimum wage rates for young people; Spain does not, and Greece only for workers in new jobs (see OECD 2015).

While comparing the effect of national wage levels in neighbouring European countries does not offer the same "natural experiments" of their effects as in neighbouring US states – because economic and regulatory conditions can be so different across national borders – evidence within European countries over time has demonstrated some tangible effects, particularly for young workers, where there is rapid change.

A clear-cut example is the experience of Portugal after a minimum wage for 18- and 19-years-olds, which had been set 25 per cent below the adult rate, was abolished in 1987. This stark change, effectively raising the minimum for 18–19-year-olds by a third, produced a substantial drop in employment for this age group, and a significant although smaller associated increase in the employment of 20–25-year-olds. Importantly, there was no effect on the rest of the working age population, since the kinds of jobs affected were not usually done by adults older than 30. In this case, therefore, both an overall reduction in jobs and a degree of substitution of slightly older workers resulted from the increase (see Pereira 2003).

In Spain, on the other hand, studies in the 1980s and 1990s suggested that the effects of minimum wage increases were restricted to substitution rather than net job loss: a 10 per cent increase in the minimum wage was found to reduce youth employment between 1.5 and 6 per cent, but without an overall reduction in employment (Perez Dominguez 1995; Dolado *et al*. 1996; Gonzalez Güemez 1997). However, these studies were carried out before the abolition of youth rates in 1998, and before a politically driven increase by a third in the mid-2000s. Some authors suggested this was likely to have had a substantial effect on youth employment (Perez Dominguez & Gonzalez Güemez 2005), but there is no clear-cut empirical evidence of whether this is the case. In the 2015 and 2016 general elections, trade unions and the left wing party Podemos called for a substantial increase. This may seem ambitious, given that youth unemployment in Spain, despite having been reduced somewhat from its peak, remained above 40 per cent.

Overall, then, evidence of effects of minimum wages in Europe has been selective and far less empirically grounded than in the United States. The difficulty in collecting definitive evidence in the absence of natural experiments within countries has influenced this, and political pressures for higher wages have appeared to weigh more heavily than any real attention to evidence about their effects. The United Kingdom was the exception to this up to 2015, with the Low Pay Commission policing a cautious approach, but as referred to above, this may now be changing.

---

would be the impact on labour demand if all UK employers adopted the voluntary Living Wage in the UK (representing a "worst-case scenario", not a forecast of actual employment effects), without any youth rates, showed an overall reduction of 160,000 jobs but a reduction of 300,000 for unskilled workers aged under 21 (Lawton & Pennycook 2013). This implied that for workers not in this category, employment demand would rise by 140,000.

A contrasting strategy was adopted by the UK government when it introduced its "National Living Wage" in 2016, which sharply increases the compulsory minimum for over-25s, but not for other age groups. This has introduced a new gap between minimum wages for under-25s and over-25s, which will grow over time. Potentially this could lead to displacement in the opposite direction to the normal transfer from younger to older workers. In industries such as hotels and catering, where employment security is often low, there could be a strong incentive to stop hiring workers once they reach their 25th birthday.

There is thus no perfect solution to the alignment of wage floors with age. With or without differentiation in the rate by age, there will be cases where the pay rates and value of workers at different ages will not be perfectly aligned, causing employers to prefer to hire a worker in one age category over another.

The issue of substitution by skill level can be more complex. One possibility is that the least qualified workers are disadvantaged by pay floors that make employers more selective about whom they recruit, and also that increased labour costs make them less inclined to invest in training. Alternatively, minimum wages could encourage employers to invest in existing workers and give better incentives for workers to acquire skills and to put more effort into searching for rewarding work. Evidence on this is inconclusive, suggesting that different employers and employees have adopted different strategies (Schmitt 2013). The behaviour of both employers and employees depends on the nature of particular jobs. In some cases there will be fairly simple ways of making existing workers more productive by giving simple instruction in some new techniques. If in contrast an employer seeks better educated workers to do better paying jobs in new ways, less educated individuals may find it harder to gain employment.

Any reductions in employment may affect hours as well as jobs

The potentially harmful impact of minimum wages is sometimes expressed as "Minimum wages could cost jobs". However, it is possible that reduced demand for labour results not in a reduction in the number of jobs but rather in the number of working hours of existing employees. This is a crucial distinction when considering the desirability of minimum wages from the perspective of low paid employees. A reduction in hours but not in jobs can potentially avoid creating losers, if the size of the wage increase is proportionately higher than the reduction in hours (see Box 3.4).

Evidence on the association between wage floors and working hours in the United States has been weak and inconclusive. In the United Kingdom, there is evidence that the introduction of a national minimum wage in 1999 caused about one in ten workers whose pay it affected to reduce their hours, (Stewart & Swaffield 2002) and that the average reduction for all workers whose pay was affected (including those with no change in hours) was between one and two hours a week (Stewart & Swaffield 2004).

BOX 3.4 WHY BETTER PAY BUT LOWER EMPLOYMENT MAY AVOID CREATING LOSERS

Arguments about wage floors tend to assume that they are counterproductive if they reduce employment. But should the combination of higher pay and less work always be seen as harmful? One issue, raised earlier in this chapter, is the strength of this effect: if many people are better paid, a very small reduction in employment may be seen as a price worth paying. A further point to consider is whether it needs to harm anyone, if the cut in employment is shared around.

If Jim gets a pay increase but as a result Jane has no job, there is a winner and a loser. If Jim and Jane both get pay increases but their working hours reduce, both will be winners, as long as total pay rises. This will be the case as long as the percentage increase in pay exceeds the percentage reduction in hours. In economic terms, this is expressed as elasticity of demand for labour being between 0 and –1. Note that where elasticities have been estimated (see above), they have been only a fraction of this amount – that is, the amount of work falls proportionately much less than hourly pay increases. Note also that the benefit to workers in this case is not just that total pay increases to make them financially better off, but also that they have more leisure time – an important consideration for people who may have had to work long hours to make ends meet, or who are juggling working and caring responsibilities.

Higher wage costs may be offset by lower staff turnover

Higher wages may be expected to increase the cost of labour for employers, but this effect may be modified by changes in the cost of employing people other than wage costs. In low-paying sectors, which tend to be typified by high staff turnover, the cost of hiring people may be substantial. This can be felt in a number of ways, including the costs of advertising a job, the greater cost of running the human resources department, the impact on business of having an empty post for a time and the lower output of a new worker while they are being inducted or trained. Reducing turnover rates can thus produce substantial gains. When workers feel that they are adequately paid, they are less likely to seek work elsewhere, and this may also be influenced by a sense that they are being more valued, especially where voluntary "living wage employers" proclaim this status as a sign of caring about their workers.

The same United States studies that have found limited employment differences in restaurants in neighbouring counties in states with different minimum wages have also found that turnover rates fall substantially following a minimum wage increase (Dube *et al.* 2010). They have found similar results in publicly contracted services where living wage ordinances have been imposed. Evidence in the United Kingdom also highlights staff turnover as the single most important change associated with introducing a voluntary living wage, with absenteeism also falling. One study for example (Wills & Linneker 2012) found that in a sample of London employers taking up the Living Wage, turnover had reduced by an average of 25 per cent, although in light of small sample sizes these results must be taken as indicative. Another UK study, examining data on pay rates and job changes, found that when the national minimum wage increases, those who benefit the most have a relatively high chance of remaining in their job compared to those with a smaller or no benefit (Dickson & Papps 2016).

Higher wage costs are sometimes passed on to consumers through price

One way for a firm to pay people more is to increase its prices. In a completely free market, this may not be an option, because the firm will be undercut by a competitor paying lower wages and charging lower prices. However where all employers in a country or state must pay a minimum wage, this undercutting is no longer possible, at least from employers covered by the same rules. If competition goes beyond these boundaries, for example in goods traded internationally, there is still a problem. However, most low-paid jobs are in "non-exportable" jobs in service industries. If a fast-food restaurant raises its prices because wages must be higher in the local area, another worker living hundreds of miles away cannot produce the same service more cheaply from a distance.

In both the United Kingdom and the United States, there is evidence that part of the cost of raising minimum wages has been passed on to consumers. The most extensive study of this subject in the UK (Wadsworth 2007) suggests that after the introduction of the national minimum wage, prices rose by 0.8 per cent a year faster than average in affected industries. This evidence also rejects a theory that such an effect neutralizes the benefit of better pay, because low-paid workers tend to consume services (such as pub drinks and takeaway food) produced by other low-paid workers. This is true for some low-paid industries, but for others, such as dry cleaning and hairdressing, the reverse is true, so higher prices have fairly even effects across the population. In the United States, a review of the evidence also showed a distinct but small price effect, suggesting that increasing a minimum wage by 10 per cent raises general prices by about 0.4 per cent (Lemos 2008).

The effects may depend on the state of the economy

One difficulty with considering overall effects of evidence on wage floors is that they have been carried out in different places and at different times, when conditions may affect the outcome in different ways. This is especially important because economists so often draw on the past to try to forecast the future. At any one time, the economy is operating in a unique context which has never been experienced before, requiring caution in making such projections.

It is perhaps not coincidental that some of the most significant increases in minimum wages have come in good economic times. Reflecting on substantial increases in minimum wages implemented in the 1990s, the chair of President Bill Clinton's Council of Economic Advisors, Laura d'Andrea Tyson, commented: "a higher minimum wage did not impede robust employment growth; it did contribute to healthy income gains for low-wage workers" (Tyson 2013).

In contrast, some studies have reported higher risks to jobs of raising the minimum wage during a recession. It is important to note that such studies do not show a general effect on jobs, even when the economy is weak, but rather that there may be effects in areas where job prospects are already relatively low. For example one study (Addison *et al.* 2013) found that in the United States from 2007 to 2009, employment effects were seen only in states where unemployment was high. Another study (Gorry 2013) comparing the US and France suggested that in the latter, the impact of the minimum wage on jobs in recession had a greater employment effect because of a higher unemployment baseline. Such evidence does therefore show that any increase in a wage floor during a recession will cost jobs, but that its impact must be looked at carefully in combination with other conditions, particularly to avoid further harm to groups who already have a weak position in the labour market.

Publicly contracted labour markets may operate differently

A private employer raising the wages of low-paid workers faces a range of choices, including producing less, raising prices and changing the nature of their product. For public employers and firms supplying services to the public sector, the options may be different. For a public body directly employing labour, "raising the price" may not be an option where tax revenues are fixed. There may also be a legal obligation to supply a certain amount of a service to the public, although the quality of this service may be hard to enforce. On the other hand, some effects of better pay noted above can apply across sectors, including the benefits of lower staff turnover and the incentive to take measures to increase staff productivity.

For private contractors, being required to pay a "living wage" may encourage more competitive bidding for contracts, as well as pruning profit margins. On the other hand, contractors may also pass on higher costs to public clients. Just as private companies being forced to pay a higher minimum wage can raise prices without fear of lower-paying competitors undercutting them, so bidders for public contracts may increase their fees on this basis. Indeed, research in this area suggests that many bidders welcome the "level playing field", and the chance to bid on the basis of a high quality service rather than low price based on low pay (Brenner 2004). Overall, this research shows that there have at most been very modest increases in city contracting costs in the United States.

In the United Kingdom, on the other hand, the projected 38 per cent increase in minimum wages for over-25s between 2015 and 2020 (see Chapter 2) is likely to bring a very specific problem to one area of public contracting: social care. This sector has a high proportion of low-paid workers, relatively few aged under 25 and limited opportunities for improving productivity, at least in the short term. Previous evidence (Machin *et al.* 2003) showed that when the UK first introduced a minimum wage in 1999, this caused many of its workers to get substantial pay rises, and that employment appeared to fall, although by relatively little considering the magnitude of pay increases. After the introduction of the "National Living Wage" brought another steep pay hike for many care workers in 2016, there was an increased "bunching" of their pay rates around this wage floor, as there had been in 1999, bringing the proportion of care workers on the statutory minimum up to one in three. The higher this proportion, the bigger the impact of further increases on the overall pay bill. There had not by 2016 been any further noticeable effect on employment levels. However, with public budgets tight and the compulsory wage still set to increase steeply, existing service levels and employment rates in the sector will become increasingly difficult to sustain.

Workers earning above a wage floor could be affected in various ways

The most obvious direct effect of a minimum or living wage is to dictate the pay rate of anyone who might otherwise have earned below the level set. Raising a minimum wage to $10 an hour means people previously paid $9 will earn $10. But what about people previously paid $11 an hour? Three outcomes are possible. Either their pay could remain at $11, causing a "flattening" of pay structures. If $9 an hour workers had been supervised by people on $11, the difference between their wages will halve, from $2 to $1. This may reduce incentives to seek promotion and make people taking on more responsibilities think that they are being poorly rewarded for doing so. To avoid this, employers may alternatively seek to preserve a differential of $2, raising supervisors' pay to $12, or by a smaller amount in order to reduce the effect on differentials. The opposite effect would be to cut back on better-paid workers' wages, in order to help cover the cost of the minimum wage increase. While they are unlikely to reduce supervisors' pay directly (for example to $10.50), they may avoid increasing it over time as they might otherwise have done, causing further convergence of pay at different grades as the minimum wage rises to cover inflation. Which of these strategies is adopted has significant effect for opportunities for lower-paid workers and their ability to progress to better living standards.

A survey of employers' intentions after the announcement of the UK's "National Living Wage" in 2015 suggests that in practice higher wage floors will have varied effects on wages above the floor, rather than pushing them in any single direction (CIPD 2016). Faced with an immediate prospect of an increased minimum wage for over-25s by more than 10 per cent in the first year and further increases in the pipeline, only 9 per cent of employers envisaged reducing the rate of pay growth for the rest of the workforce. Greater proportions thought they would help cover the extra cost of the higher minimum in other ways such as raising efficiency or productivity (30%), taking lower profits or absorbing the costs (22%) or raising prices (15%). On the other hand, somewhat more employers (26%) thought that they would reduce differentials between workers affected by the National Living Wage and their supervisors or managers than employers who thought that they would preserve such differentials (20%). (Half of those surveyed had not yet decided what to do.)

If the long-term effect of higher wage floors is to cause a flatter wage structure among lower-paid jobs, this could be looked at in one of two ways. On the one hand, it could be seen as exacerbating a trend known as the "hollowing out" of the labour market, whereby there are more well-paid and poorly paid but fewer medium-paid jobs than in the past. Some highly educated workers are well paid for their sought-after skills in the "knowledge economy"; others without these skills provide low-value routine services (such as shelf-stacking) at low pay. Higher pay floors could undermine jobs in the middle, such as supervisory jobs, by causing employers to focus on pay for the least skilled. On the other hand, in order to make it viable to hire such workers at the higher rate, there will be pressure to increase their skills and productivity. Thus, while such a policy will not restore the jobs in the middle, it could help transform the jobs at the bottom, narrowing the gap that has opened up between well-paid and poorly paid employment.

Commentary

Few aspects of economic theory have had as great an influence as the idea that an attempt to set wages at a fixed minimum will be counterproductive because those able to command the lowest wages in the market will then become unemployed. Yet decades of research have failed to confirm this theory in practice. Some economists stick to the theory, pointing to certain cases where it appears to have been accurate, and warning of the risks of ignoring it. Others argue that the theory needs to be adapted to the way in which labour markets actually work.

Some have tried to build alternative models from the "neoclassical" relationship shown in the graphs at the start of this chapter. For example, they suggest that, while labour markets are not as monopsonistic (dominated by a single local employer) as they may have been when one company could dominate employment in a town, there are still "frictions" that prevent them from operating completely freely. By this they mean that while workers are not obliged to stay with one employer, changing jobs has enough difficulties to allow firms to set wages lower than they would if workers were perfectly mobile. However, any effort to model the effects of such markets cannot represent a universal reality as in the simple model, since conditions vary greatly from case to case.

Rather than a single set of rules about the effect of wage floors on labour markets, then, the evidence points to a series of ways in which employers and workers may respond. These include reducing working hours, making labour more productive (either with the same set of workers or through different hiring practices) and raising prices. Other knock-on effects may be to diminish profits or reduce staff turnover.

Some of these impacts may be wholly benign. If wages can be increased without raising labour costs because staff become more loyal and recruitment costs decrease, everybody wins. If paying a decent wage encourages employers to find ways of using labour more effectively, additional costs will be offset. Often, though, the effects involve winners and losers. While workers will be net winners if they end up working fewer hours for more total pay, this is likely to reduce profits, and thus represents some loss in revenue to shareholders or company owners. If minimum wages drive up prices, the workers in the industries affected gain at the expense of its consumers. In both of these cases, this may be seen as justified – because low-paid workers are seen as being exploited to allow holders of capital to make unusual profits through market power, and by providing services to consumers at unjustifiably low prices.

Thus, paying workers enough to live on comes back to a moral choice with consequences for the distribution of economic well-being. But can pay floors truly be effective in ensuring that workers and their families have enough – as suggested by the paradigm of a "living wage"? This depends on the interaction between a worker's wage and the overall income of their household, which is affected by many other factors as well as wage rates. Chapter 4 therefore puts the living wage debate in the wider context of approaches to tackling low income.

4

Interactions with incomes and social policy

How much do you earn? Many of us would like to ask this question of our friends (though it is often a taboo), for two main reasons. One is because we are curious about how highly they are valued by their employers. The other is because it gives us a clue to what kind of living standard they can afford. When we think in these terms, we often consider wages, earnings and incomes as interchangeable concepts.

In fact, they are not, and it is helpful to distinguish each, and to think about how they relate to each other. My hourly *wage* rate perhaps best represents how much my employer values my work (I may not be paid hourly, but an annual *salary* expresses something similar – the full-time rate for my job). On the other hand, my *earnings* over a week, month or year depend on both my wage rate and on how many hours I work; and my family's earnings are the result of how much we work collectively, as well as the wage rates of each of us who work. This helps determine our overall household *income*, which expresses how much money we have coming in. However, what we earn is not the whole story, since income is best thought about net of taxes, and includes "unearned" elements such as benefits, pensions and investment returns. Another feature of income is that it can be adjusted for household size when thinking about whether it is high enough to meet people's needs, or whether it is too low to escape poverty (see Box 4.1).

As a consequence of all these steps from an hourly wage to a household income, two people working side-by-side on the same wage rate may enjoy very different living standards. This makes the concept of a "living wage" far from straightforward. It is at best a simplified approximation, using methods described in Chapter 2, of what wage tends to produce adequate income levels, given prevailing family and working patterns.

The imperfect relationship between wages and incomes raises three key questions, which this chapter considers in turn. First of all, to what extent

BOX 4.1 ADJUSTING INCOME FOR HOUSEHOLD COMPOSITION

Income is generally measured at the level of the household. A household is a family or other group of people who live together and share at least some living expenses. This pooling of resources makes an overall figure for household income more appropriate than thinking about what one individual earns. Nevertheless, we should bear in mind that looking at household income as if it were fully pooled is a simplification. Studies have shown, for example, that whether money coming into the family is paid to the mother or the father can influence what and whom it is spent on.

A measure of household income combines all income received by members of a household, net of income taxes. But clearly, the living standard that a given level of household income produces varies with the size of household: an income of $30,000 a year will make you much better off if you live alone than if you support a family of six. When measuring income distribution, therefore, it is conventional to "equivalize" incomes by multiplying them by a factor related to the household's composition. This allows an adjusted set of incomes to be compared. Typically, the scales used to make this adjustment assume that to reach a given living standard, a single person requires an income about two thirds as high as that of a couple (not half as high, since it is more economical, per person, to share costs). Additional children are assumed to cost less than additional adults. "Equivalization" has added an ugly word to the English dictionary, but a useful tool to economic analysis.

do people who are low paid live in low income households? This sets the context in which better pay can be used as a tool to help workers avoid low income and poverty.

Second, what is the evidence in practice that better wage floors (the payment of living wages or the raising of minimum wages) have actually improved the lives of workers and their families?

And third, how do living wages relate to wider policies to improve low incomes? This is perhaps the most important public policy issue discussed in this book, not least because of the limited success in recent years of policies seeking to tackle poverty and low income, yet the considerable impact of living wage movements.

This is perhaps the most important public policy issue discussed in this book, not least because at the same time as the impact of living wage movements has grown, some other policies to tackle poverty and low income have faltered. It also makes selective references to other countries, particularly the United States.

The overlap between low pay and low income

A century ago, when family income depended heavily on full-time male breadwinners, it was reasonable to assume that families supported by low-paid men would usually have low living standards, and that setting a reasonable wage floor would go a long way towards addressing working poverty.

Today, family and working patterns are more complex. Most women work, whether contributing an amount to family income lower than, equal to or greater than a male partner, or being the sole breadwinner in the case of a single person or lone parent: about six in ten women aged 15–64 in Europe and the United States are working, not much lower than the seven in ten men who do so. Part-time working has become more common, greatly affecting the impact of a given wage on family income. And in families with young children where both parents or a single parent work, childcare requirements and costs can be as important as wage rates in determining final disposable income.

In one respect, these changes have actually strengthened the link between minimum pay rates and family living standards. Families depend to a greater extent for their incomes on women's wages than in the past, and women have always been more likely than men to be low paid. In the past, women's wages were often regarded as supplementary to men's in supporting families, sometimes described as "pin money": a bit of additional income to buy non-essential extras. This was used as an argument against a universal minimum wage, and sometimes for applying it to men only. Today, women are still over-represented in low-paying occupations, such as care work, but they are also working more, and many are supporting families on their own. If their pay is low, this matters a lot for their families' living standards.

On the other hand, variability in the hours of both individuals and households can influence living standards just as much today as hourly wage rates. The proportion of employees who are part-time has grown steadily, to nearly one in three in the UK. And working patterns in families have become more diverse. In 1975, for every 20 working families with children in the UK, twelve fit the traditional model of a father working and a mother staying at home. Only one was a lone parent; in the other seven, both parents worked. Today, only five out of twenty working families fit the "single male breadwinner" model, four are lone parents and the majority (eleven) have both parents working.

This diversification of family working patterns means that families with the most difficulty making ends meet are not just those with the lowest hourly wages, but often those with the fewest or least stable working hours. A lone parent, say, working in a supermarket for on average 20 hours a week at 20 per cent above the minimum wage will have lower earnings than a single person flipping burgers for 30 hours a week paid the minimum. Her wages will also be considerably less adequate relative to her family needs than a single person who does not have to support children. A significantly higher wage floor would help the burger-flipper but do little or nothing to help the supermarket worker, who would be better helped by being able to work more hours or getting extra help from the state targeted at workers with low incomes relative to family size. In other words, because very low pay is often not the cause of working poverty, raising a pay floor will not help everyone in this situation.

Looking more precisely at the overlap between low pay and low income is not very easy. Data on individuals and their wages tends to be collected separately from those on households and their incomes. Even where they can be combined, they are not easy to interpret. It is possible to identify households that contain at least one person paid the minimum wage at some point over a given period. What is harder is to work out people's average hourly pay rates from their reported earnings, especially if they work variable, part-time hours. Data is therefore most commonly reported on full-time workers, but they are inherently less likely than part-timers to have low income. Despite these limitations, studies that have looked in various ways at the overlap between low pay and low income (see for example Maitre *et al.* 2012; Nolan & Marx 2000; Brewer *et al.* 2009) have produced three interesting observations:

- First, the overlap between low pay and low income is much greater in some countries than in others. It has tended to be higher in the United States, where both wage and income inequalities are relatively high, than in Europe. In other words, where low-paid workers are particularly poorly paid compared to high-paid ones, this has a more marked effect on the income distribution, regardless of other influences such as working hours. Low-wage workers find it harder to escape poverty, even by working longer hours.

- Second, however, there are no recorded cases of developed countries where most low-paid workers are in poverty, or where one in five of the poorest 20 per cent of households. The great majority of workers, low paid or not, are better off than this.
- Third, on the other hand, the great majority of those workers who are on very low or fairly low incomes *are* in fact low paid.

This combination of findings may sound odd. How is it possible that most low-paid workers are not in poverty, but most workers in poverty are low paid? The answer to this paradox is crucial in understanding the potential role of pay floors in addressing low income.

The explanation is illustrated in the two graphs shown in Figure 4.1. The first graph shows that for a particular group of UK low-paid workers, full-timers, the risk of being on very low household income is smaller than the chance of being in the middle of the income distribution. This is because simply the fact of working full-time gives you a head start over the 50 per cent of working age adults who either work part-time or not at all, so only one in five of the poorest households include a full-time worker. If it were possible to have the same graph for all individuals who work, including part-timers, we would expect from other evidence to see low-paid workers most commonly in the second poorest fifth, rather than in the middle of the distribution, but still not in the bottom fifth, which is dominated by those not working.

Nevertheless, it can be seen from the first graph that the workers who do end up on relatively low incomes are predominantly those who are low paid. This is brought out more clearly in the second graph, which includes only full-time workers. Clearly, an increase in wages would help these households to improve their relatively low living standards. Many families, despite having someone in work, struggle to make ends meet, and a disproportionate number of these have members on low pay. Specifically, according to the UK's Minimum Income Standard described in Chapter 2, which considers what households require for an acceptable standard of living that allows them to participate in society, 30 per cent of the population now have

(a)

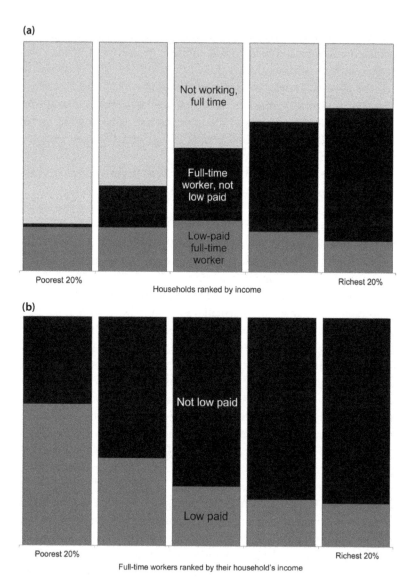

Figure 4.1 Household income status of individuals by work and pay status, 2014–15. (a) All working-age adults, relative income distribution across households; (b) only full-time workers.

Low pay defined as below two-thirds median earnings.

Source: author calculations from Family Resources Survey

incomes below that standard (a figure that has increased from 25% before the 2009 recession). Many of these have low-paid workers, and for these families, a pay increase may make a significant difference in enabling them to make ends meet.

Thus, while most low-paid workers are not in dire poverty, many are finding it hard to achieve the kind of acceptable living standard that living wages seek to provide.

It is also important to note that low pay and low income overlap to different degrees for different types of household. Not surprisingly, they overlap the most for those with only one worker – a single person, lone parent or couple where just one person works. Having a partner who works helps many low-paid workers avoid low income, while having more dependants makes low income more likely. Workers under 30 are more likely to be low paid, but also significantly more likely to live with other people who are earning (most obviously with parents) than are older workers. Women are also more likely to be low paid, but low-paid women are less likely than low-paid men to be in poverty, again because of the earnings of those they live with (Maitre *et al.* 2012).

To sum up this picture of the overlap between low pay and low income: being low paid puts you at greater risk of not having the household income needed to participate in society, and the many working people who find it hardest to make ends meet are principally low paid. However, the risks are unsurprisingly greatest for those low-paid workers whose households are most dependent on their earnings, while some groups such as young adults living with their parents may not have low family income as a result of low pay. The conclusion must be that a wage floor is likely to be important for some groups more than for others in supporting an adequate living standard.

How effectively do higher wage floors secure adequate living standards?

A pay rise will almost always make someone better off. (An exception would be if it caused them to cross a threshold of eligibility for some help from the state, such as free school meals, worth more than the increase in pay.) But how effective are living wages or higher minimum wages in improving the lives of low income households? This will be influenced by a range of factors:

- First, the extent to which families with low living standards include workers with wages low enough to be affected by such an increase. As shown above, most low income families do not include a low-paid worker, so we must start by acknowledging that it will only be a partial solution to low income.
- Second, the strength of the "lighthouse effect": the tendency of a higher minimum to cause an increase in other wages somewhat above this minimum. This means that some people on low pay but not the lowest pay may benefit, affecting a wider range of low-income working families than just those with workers on very low pay.
- Third, and very importantly, the extent to which additional earnings translate into additional household income. This can be reduced by the taxation of income and by the reduction of family benefits that are means-tested against income. As discussed later in this chapter, many countries have been making increasing use of in-work benefits that help low-earning families make ends meet through a state transfer that reduces as earnings rise. This offers protection against very low income among such families, but also means that any pay rise may be partially "clawed back" through a reduction in benefits.

The United States and the United Kingdom both have tax credit systems that offer such means-tested benefits to working families. However, they operate in significantly different ways (see Box 4.2). In the United Kingdom, maximum tax credits are much higher than in the United States, but the entitlement declines much faster with rising income. The consequence is that the potential for families with children to improve their income through raises in pay is much greater in the US than in the UK. Another way of looking at this is that the tax credit system does more to help families escape poverty, whereas in the United State, escaping poverty is more contingent on wages being adequate.

In the UK, the state's high clawback of benefits for people receiving pay increases does not make living wages irrelevant to escaping low income. A study of beneficiaries of the London Living Wage (Wills & Linneker 2012) found that most did not receive tax credits, either because they did not have

BOX 4.2 TAX CREDITS AND THE EFFECT OF PAY INCREASES IN THE UNITED KINGDOM AND THE UNITED STATES

Since the 1970s, the governments of both the United Kingdom and the United States have helped working families on low incomes to make ends meet by topping up their wages. These payments, come in the form of tax credits (and in the UK the new Universal Credit, being phased in at time of writing). Such a tax credit can take the form of a regular cheque from the state, or a reduction in tax liabilities, for families eligible because their incomes are low.

The different ways in which tax credits are structured in the UK and US, shown in Figures 4.2 and 4.3, have important effects on the ability of increases in wages to improve living standards in the short term. In the United Kingdom, a family on very low earnings gets a substantial entitlement under Universal Credit, the same as if they were out of work, which includes an allowance for rented housing. However, once they are earning a small amount – equivalent to just six hours a week earned on the National Living Wage – this starts to be withdrawn rapidly. For every pound the family earns, it loses 65p in Universal Credit, so ends up only 35p better off. This means for example that an

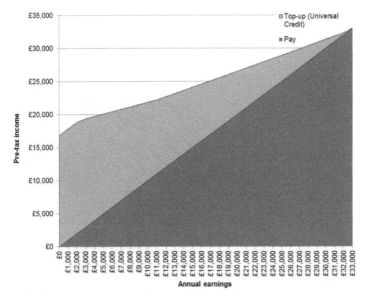

Figure 4.2 Pay and universal credit (UK) for single-earner couple with two children in social housing, 2016.

announcement in 2015 that the minimum wage for over-25s would increase substantially, by around £2.80 an hour over the following five years, would for someone getting Universal Credit actually amount only to just under £1 an hour if they were below the income tax threshold, or 70p an hour if paying tax - meaning the worker would keep only a quarter of their gross pay rise.

For an American worker on the federal minimum wage entitled to the Earned Income Tax Credit (EITC), things look very different. The EITC does much less than Universal Credit to get a very low earning worker out of poverty, but does much more to incentivize work. In doing so, it allows workers to keep a much greater portion of a pay increase. In fact, for someone with two children and family earnings up to $13,930 a year, the EITC increases with rising pay. Since this is equivalent to about 37 hour' work a week on the federal minimum wage, any parent working less than full-time who does not have a working partner gains $1.40 for every $1 pay increase. Above that level, the EITC remains stable up to $18,190 for a lone parent and $23,740 for a couple, after which it reduces much more slowly than in the UK: by around 21 cents for each extra dollar earned.

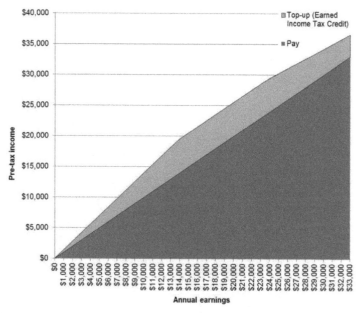

Figure 4.3 Pay and earned income tax credit (USA) for single-earner couple with two children, 2016.

children, had household income too high to be eligible or did not claim. There was also a preference for receiving income through the pay packet rather than through means-tested benefits. Nevertheless, the limited effects of pay increases on the net income of low income families claiming tax credits cannot be ignored when considering their ability to reduce family poverty.

Research in the US suggests that higher minimum wages or living wage ordinances systematically reduce poverty rates. A survey of this research shows that almost all studies confirm this relationship, and its author estimates that for each 10 per cent increase in the minimum wage, poverty reduces by 2.4 per cent in the short term and 3.6 per cent in the long term (Dube 2013). This meant that a proposal to raise the minimum wage from $7.25 to $10.10 would have reduced poverty by around 14 per cent, or 6.8 million people. This study also found that increasing the minimum wage had the greatest effect on average incomes low down the income distribution (10 per cent from the bottom), but for those at the 30th percentile (with incomes higher than 30% of the population and lower than 70%), there was no measurable effect.

In the United Kingdom, evidence suggests that effects are less focused on people on the lowest incomes, influenced strongly by the smaller net gains experienced by those on means-tested benefits as shown in Box 4.2. The findings of a study considering what would be the impact on households with different incomes of paying the accredited voluntary living wage to all workers (Lawton & Pennycook 2013) is shown in Figure 4.4. In absolute terms, the average benefit is greatest for people in the middle of the income distribution, but in proportional terms (as a percentage of each household's income), it is strongest at the bottom. This means that even though benefits would be spread across the income distribution, the overall effect would be "redistributive", producing a more equal distribution of incomes.

Thus, whole-economy studies of effects of wage floors on poverty and the income distribution show distinct effects, although these are less clear-cut in the United Kingdom than the United States. While it is important to try to estimate these overall effects, the reality is that the impact of minimum or living wages on individuals will vary immensely in different cases. The most striking evidence of their effects can be highly specific and localized. As shown in Chapters 1 and 2 of this book, the case for living wages has often originated from the situation of a particular group of exploited workers,

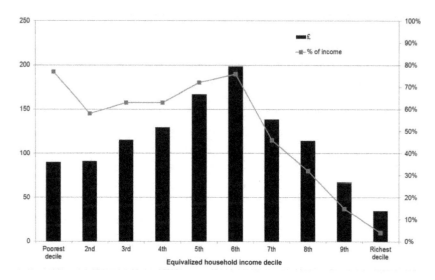

Figure 4.4 Average change in annual net household income if all employees were paid at least the living wage, all households, 2008–9 (in 2012 prices).

Source: Lawton & Pennycook (2013), with thanks to Resolution Foundation for data

whether those working in the sweatshops of the industrial revolution, or in insecure, poorly paid service jobs contracted to the public sector in the twenty-first century. Box 4.3 gives a striking example of how the lives of care workers in San Francisco were transformed by living wages.

These benefits can be seen not just narrowly in terms of income, but also in terms of improving well-being more widely. Some US studies suggest for example that raising minimum pay can have significant effects in improving outcomes such as health. For example, the Living Wage Ordinance in San Francisco has been associated with less sickness absence, improved subjective health and reduced premature death rates (Bhatia & Katz 2001). A UK study found that those who received the London Living Wage scored 3.9 units higher on a 70-point well-being scale than those who did not, controlling for other socio-economic and demographic characteristics (Flint *et al.* 2013). While a pay rise in itself may not bring such benefits, workers in low-paid sectors with living wage employers appear to gain a greater sense of well-being in their working lives, linked to feeling valued by their employers, sometimes receiving more training and developing greater loyalty associated with changing jobs less frequently.

BOX 4.3 THE TRANSFORMATION OF THE LIVES OF SAN FRANCISCO'S HOME CARE WORKERS

The effect of a wage increase on a group of workers' lives can often be hard to pin down. People working alongside each other go home to very different situations, with multiple influences on their well-being and living standards. However, the potential for wage increases to be transformative was demonstrated by a particularly large increase for a significant group of workers between 1997 and 2001: home carers in San Francisco. Over this period, the combination of the city's Living Wage Ordinance and union bargaining caused pay of these workers, previously very low, almost to double, to over $10 an hour.

The workforce in this industry was ethnically diverse, with a high proportion of immigrants and mainly female employees. An important effect of the wage increase was to draw many more people in these communities into this kind of work, rather than working in factories, restaurants and hotels. It also provided a more attractive alternative to those industries for people transitioning from welfare to work, under programmes running at this time. Staff turnover rates dropped, with a 30 per cent fall in the number of departures above what would be a normal rate of turnover. This in turn increased the supply of "good" providers of suitable care, improving the quality of the service. For the populations who benefited, living standards improved substantially, and it is estimated that the movement of low-paid workers into this sector, combined with gains for existing workers, could have reduced poverty in San Francisco by as much as 15 per cent (see Howes 2002).

Wage floors and policies to tackle low income

A living wage by definition seeks to improve living standards of those who receive it. Yet as this chapter has shown, low pay and low income overlap, but are very different. Many people receiving a pay rise under a living wage do not have low household income, perhaps because other people in their household earn well. Many households in poverty do not have anyone with low wages, either because nobody in their household works or because they work on reasonable pay but for few hours.

As a consequence, policies seeking to address poverty directly have focused mainly on improving household incomes among targeted groups, rather than tackling low pay. One way of doing so has been to try to get more people into work, especially among groups such as lone parents where worklessness and poverty are closely linked. Another strategy has been to extend the scope of cash benefits for people on low incomes. These have traditionally been available mainly for people out of work, but increasingly are available to working families, under tax credits and other forms of support. Means-tested support for working families, topping up their wages, have been around for over four decades in the United States and the United Kingdom (see Box 4.2 above), but have grown in importance in those countries, and spread to other countries. They have been especially strong in English-speaking countries, where general family benefits have been relatively weak, and where widening wage inequalities and the growth of lone parenthood have left many families unable to make a living through wages alone. More recently, many continental European countries, such as Austria, Belgium and France, have supplemented their relatively generous benefits available to all families with additional income-related cash benefits or tax breaks for working families on low incomes (Marx & Nelson 2013).

The growth of in-work benefits has opened up an important debate about the respective roles of employers and governments in securing acceptable living standards.

Some people argue that when governments top-up wages to allow working families to avoid poverty they are simply encouraging low pay, allowing employers to pay "poverty wages", subsidized by taxpayers. Others argue against relying on wages to meet social objectives. Some free market advocates make this argument from the perspective of not interfering in the labour market by fixing wage floors, and prefer the government to intervene through redistribution to top-up incomes (Bourne 2015). Caution about the living wage is also shared by commentators who fear that its prominence might falsely suggest that poverty and low income can be addressed principally through wages, and thus distract from more targeted and effective approaches (e.g. Bennett 2014).

These arguments have come into sharp focus in the United Kingdom in recent years, with the growth of and challenge to tax credits. This story and its precursors help illustrate dilemmas in addressing in-work poverty.

Wages and state support for working families in the UK: past, present and future

The idea of using public money to keep working people on low pay out of poverty is far from new in the UK. It was first tried in what became known as the "Speenhamland" system of the late eighteenth and early nineteenth centuries. This was an agreement by local authorities to combat rural poverty by using local rates paid by landowners to top-up pay to a level determined by the price of bread and the number of children a family had to feed. However, in the recession that followed the Napoleonic Wars, employers exploited this system to cut pay, leading to a growing burden on the rate-paying landowners and eventually a reduction in entitlements – leaving workers worse off. Eventually, the system was scrapped by the 1834 Poor Law, which replaced income top-ups with the repressive workhouse as the only option for workers unable to reach a subsistence income by their own means (see Wilkinson 2001).

As outlined in Chapter 1, the low pay and low living standards experienced by many workers in the nineteenth century led to calls for a living/minimum wage, but were more effectively addressed in the twentieth century by collective bargaining. However, anti-poverty campaigners such as Elfrida Rathbone in the 1920s pointed out that the adequacy of wages in meeting family needs depended on the size of the family, and argued for family allowances to help provide for the additional cost of children. This case was taken up by William Beveridge in his famous (1942) report proposing a new system of social protection. As a result, in addition to wages, those with children gained family allowances, and later Child Benefit – paid regardless of other income, to help cover the cost of a child. However, while these payments helped equalize the welfare of people on a given wage with different family responsibilities, they never did so fully, and these benefits have tended to decline relative to the cost of bringing up a child.

From about 1979, child poverty started to grow rapidly (doubling over the next decade), influenced by these child benefit cuts, by growing wage inequality and by a growth in lone parenthood. In-work top-ups had been reintroduced at a modest level in 1971, and grew over the following decades into the present tax credit system, now being replaced by Universal Credit. While there have been five different versions of this system (Family Income Supplement, Family Credit, Working Families Tax Credit, Child/Working

Tax Credit and Universal Credit), there has been considerable continuity in their structure. Most significantly, they help "make work pay" and reduce working poverty by ensuring that people are better off in work than on out-of-work benefits, but at the same time are sharply withdrawn with rising earnings, so that the benefits of working extra hours or getting a pay rise are muted.

Following four decades in which the value of these top-ups had broadly increased, they became the target of government cuts from 2011 onwards. It could be argued that this echoed what had happened two centuries earlier, when the "Speenhamland" top-ups had become too expensive to maintain in an economy dominated by low wages that they had helped to encourage. In this sense, the warm embrace of a government income guarantee may be a mixed blessing for families, insofar as it encourages pay to remain low, which helps make the guarantee too expensive for the state to maintain, and in times of public austerity, makes its recipients vulnerable to cuts in state benefits on which they have come to depend.

In 2015, the government narrative on making work pay changed fundamentally. Up until then, the message to disadvantaged families had been something like: "we will make it worth your while to work, by ensuring that your wages, however modest, are topped up to a specified level". However, a growth in the number of children whose parents worked but were still in poverty suggested that this policy was not working well. In announcing the National Living Wage, a much higher compulsory minimum for workers over 25 (see Chapter 2), the Chancellor of the Exchequer George Osborne expressed his intention of moving from a "low wage, high tax, high welfare economy; to [a] higher wage, lower tax, lower welfare country" (Osborne 2015). In other words, he wanted wages to do more of the heavy lifting of securing acceptable living standards, rather than relying on the state.

This kind of shift can make perfect sense, if applied within realistic limits, but it can damage living standards if applied clumsily. In introducing the new approach, Mr Osborne cut tax credits at the same time as increasing the wage floor. The problem was that the reductions in support were shown to outweigh the wage increase to such a large extent for the families affected that these cuts soon had to be abandoned for political reasons.

This episode raised issues not just about the magnitude of cuts, but also a more fundamental question of how to implement the ambition of reducing reliance on state help by increasing wage income. This can be done with "carrots" (increasing wages) or with "sticks" (reducing in-work benefit entitlements). What should be the balance between the two?

This choice can be illustrated by Figure 4.5, which superimposes on the earlier illustration of the Universal Credit system the effects of increasing a wage and of cutting in-work benefits. The first thing to note is that, by raising the minimum wage rate to a higher "living wage" without making any change in Universal Credit entitlements, the amount paid by the state to a family reduces substantially. This is because each time someone's earnings rise, their entitlement to help falls. Thus, simply by increasing the wage, the government saves money and the family becomes less dependent on help.

If, in addition, the amount of help paid to top-up a given earnings level falls as a result of government spending cuts (dotted line), two issues arise. First, this "claws back" much or all of the gain from the wage increase for the worker: in the case shown, a family is worse off (at point B) with a higher wage but reduced entitlement than they were originally (at point A), and an

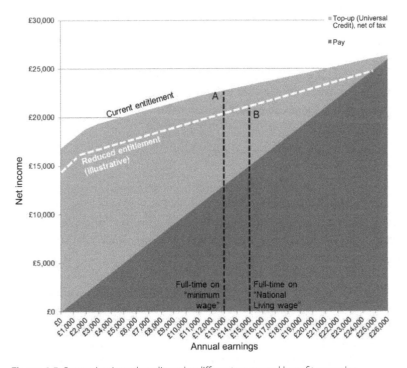

Figure 4.5 Pay and universal credit under different wage and benefit scenarios.

93

important contributing factor is the relatively small gains from higher wages resulting from the means-testing of additional earnings. Even were a full-time worker to be better off in this scenario, protection for people not able to work full-time is weakened, and someone whose circumstances restrict their earnings to a given level becomes worse off.

None of this would matter if wages could rise to a level that made it possible for families to reach an adequate living standard with no help from the state at all. However, this is not a realistic scenario for a family with children, who in most cases would need to earn significantly more than the current median wage (the wage of the worker in the middle of the distribution) in order to reach an acceptable minimum standard of living. Setting a minimum wage at this level is unlikely to be economically feasible without destroying millions of jobs.

An alternative is to see in-work benefits and a living wage not as substitutes but as complementary. The fact that the UK has decided to increase minimum wages for over-25s sharply will in itself save the government a lot of money, by moving families to the right along Figure 4.5 by increasing their pay, reducing the amount that their incomes need topping up. If this money were reinvested in Universal Credit, it would be possible to *increase* generosity, moving the top-up line upwards rather than downwards. This would help move families closer to an adequate living standard, on a given wage rate. Box 4.4 gives an example of how this could work.

Living wages and out of work benefits

While the emphasis of this chapter has been on the role that wage floors can play as part of a wider strategy to help families who work, they also need to be understood in the context of wider forms of social protection. Welfare states seek to ensure that people who lose their jobs still have a reasonable means of subsistence. This "insurance" function of benefits has created debates about whether, if they are too effective in protecting living standards, people will not have an incentive to work. This is a particular risk for those with larger families for whom out of work entitlements are large relative to what they might earn, and part of the motivation of in-work benefits based on earnings and family size is to preserve such an incentive. However, the level of wages relative to benefits is also an important factor.

BOX 4.4 HOW PAY AND BENEFITS CAN COMBINE TO REWARD A "HARD-WORKING FAMILY": AN EXAMPLE

A living wage in the UK is calculated as the wage that working households require, on average, to reach an acceptable living standard, assuming the current contribution made by the state to topping up wages. However, if the state contribution is not regarded as "given", but rather as something that needs to be considered alongside wage rates, the calculus of the living wage becomes more complex.

Politicians have been keen to emphasize that they want to encourage and reward work, so that "hard-working families" can get to a reasonable living standard. Britain's incoming Prime Minister, Theresa May, talked on taking office about helping working families who are "just about managing". But to follow through the pledge to help such families, they require both a benchmark of what standard they would like to help families attain and a narrative of how this standard can be reached. This involves a partnership between the state and employers, with each making a reasonable contribution.

Such a narrative needs some concept of how much families should have to work in order to meet their needs. Saying that a working family should have enough to live on may not be interpreted as meaning that just working a few hours a week should get you to an adequate income. On the other hand, the idea that two parents should have to work all hours in order to provide for a young family neglects the value to children of having parents with options for "work-life balance". One compromise, proposed by the Joseph Rowntree Foundation (2016: 185) in its plan to tackle poverty, is to suggest that a couple with two young children where one parent works full-time and the other half time should be able to reach a reasonable standard of living.

Figure 4.6 illustrates some options about how such a family could reach the Minimum Income Standard through a combination of wages and Universal Credit. The parallel lines show as an example what would happen if the "work allowance", the annual family earnings level above which Universal Credit starts to reduce, were raised, from its present level of £46 a week by a further £20, £40 or £60. Other policies such as varying the level of support for childcare offered by government could have similar effects. The diagram shows that at the National Minimum Wage of £6.70 an hour in 2016 (without the National Living Wage supplement paid to workers over 25), the family shown in this example would have fallen nearly £40 a week short of meeting their needs (point A). However raising the wage rate narrows but does not close this gap (point B). But if in addition to raising the wage there were also an increase in the work allowance, the gap could be closed (point C). This shows that at the target National Living Wage level, it would be possible to make the working income of this family adequate, through an increase in entitlements that would not need to be as great as if the wage were lower. Recall that part of this increase would be paid for by the reduction in Universal Credit going to families whose earnings increased because of the higher wage. In fact, the amount that the state needs to give the family at point C, topping up wages to an acceptable living standard, is about the same as at point A, where it falls a long way short. The difference is that the employer is contributing substantially more.

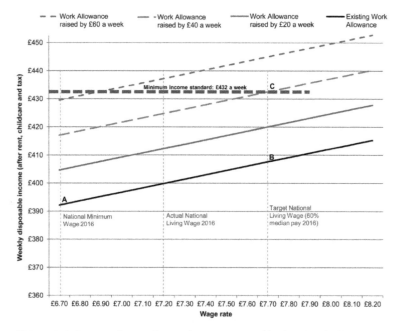

Figure 4.6 Options for combining living wage and higher "work allowance" in Universal Credit to meet Minimum Income Standard, 2016.

Work allowance is the amount you can earn before Universal Credit starts being reduced. This example is for a couple with two children, with one parent working full-time and one part-time. Assumptions include 30 hours a week of free childcare for a 4-year-old (being introduced in 2017).

European welfare states designed to offer strong insurance against severe income losses when people lose their jobs have often linked benefits closely to average earnings or minimum wages. However, as they try to maintain work incentives and also to contain public spending, there is an incentive to cut this link. When for example the Spanish government fulfilled a pledge for a steep increase in the minimum wage after 2004, it dropped its commitment to increase benefits at the same rate, creating separate systems for uprating them, as shown in Figure 4.7. Note that after rising more slowly than wages up to 2010, benefits did not rise at all in the next six years, and therefore lost value due to inflation. In the UK, uprating systems for wages and benefits have never been linked, but the 2015 commitment to increase the minimum wage for over-25s by over a third in five years contrasted starkly with a freezing of benefits and tax credits. In both Spain and the UK, this divergence means that people who lose their jobs will have a much

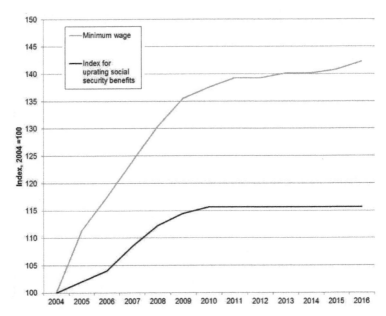

Figure 4.7 The uprating of Spanish minimum wages and social security benefits, 2004–16. Index: 2004 = 100.

Source: author calculations using data from the Spanish Ministry of Employment and Social Security (www.seg-social.es)

greater fall in their living standard than in the past. But those who retain them will be better off, and able to rely less on non-wage support in order to make ends meet.

Living wages, working hours and changes in the security of work

As has been noted throughout this book, setting a living wage requires some assumption about how many hours people work. The emphasis of living wage movements has therefore inevitably been on ensuring that people are paid enough to earn a decent living if they do work these hours. But being paid such a wage will not be sufficient if work is sporadic or a few hours per week. Recent descriptions of the "precariat" (people with fragile opportunities rather than stable lives including stable jobs) and the "gig economy" (work supplied on a series of one-off arrangements offering little or no security) raise two important issues relevant to minimum or living wages.

First, much attention has been given to whether such jobs are covered by a statutory minimum. A ruling by a UK employment tribunal in 2016 that Uber taxi drivers cannot be considered self-employed demonstrated how courts and public policy can help ensure that workers receive minimum wages and benefit from other advantages of employee status.

Second, however, employed or not, for workers with unstable hours, a reasonable hourly pay rate may not translate into an adequate weekly income. In any effort to improve working incomes, wages policies therefore need to be considered in tandem with policies affecting work opportunities and working patterns. It is conceivable that, were an extreme version of the gig economy to evolve, where everybody effectively sold their time as if they were a freelance contractor, the basis of a minimum adequate pay rate would need to be rethought. A music band playing a "gig" must charge taking account not just of the time spent at the venue, but also how long it took to arrange, and the "down time" in-between engagements. If most workers similarly became freelancers in which the number of paid hours was limited relative to the total time they were available for work, a lower hours assumption and hence a higher hourly pay rate may be needed in order to maintain an expectation of an adequate living standard.

Some commentators argue that the gig economy should be seen as an opportunity, not just as a threat to workers. There is scope, for example, to overcome the dominant market position of a single local employer where workers operate as free agents and sell their services in labour markets where information flows freely via the internet. It remains to be seen, however, to what extent this will reduce the scope for employers to pay below the true market rate, or whether large firms will find new ways of achieving dominant positions as purchasers of particular types of labour, allowing them to keep pay low.

Living wages and policies to reduce costs

Living wage calculations are based on what it is reckoned currently to cost households to reach an acceptable living standard. This chapter has noted that the contribution of wages to meeting those costs may vary according to the level of other sources of income, such as state benefits. Another factor, amenable to public policy, is the responsibility of households for meeting certain costs. In the United States, the level of health care costs incurred by households has been a major political issue, strongly influenced by public policies such as the Affordable Care Act. In the United Kingdom, successive governments have contributed various amounts to the cost of childcare, in an effort to contain the costs incurred by working families. The consequences of such policies for total household costs should influence the level of the living wage. This is therefore another aspect of public policy which needs to be considered in combination with efforts to produce adequate wage floors.

How do living wages relate to the idea of a basic income?

In recent years there has been growing discussion of whether the best way of securing a minimum living standard for all citizens would be simply for the state to pay each citizen a basic income. This has raised many debates relating to the levels of taxation that would be needed, the moral justification of an unconditional payment and the advantages and drawbacks of giving a standardized payment to everybody. It is well beyond the scope of this book to explore this complex subject, but it is worth noting that such debates overlap with the ones explored in this chapter. In particular, if not all working households are able to make ends meet through pay alone, a basic income from the state is one way of seeking to make up the difference. Certainly the existence of such a payment would reduce the hourly pay rate that could be considered a "living wage", since families would be given a head start by the state in making ends meet. However, in comparison with, say, a means-tested family tax credit, a universal basic income would be less concentrated on families with the greatest needs. As is often the case when the state makes a contribution to household income, there is a tension between a system that is simple (by paying the same amount to everyone) and one that is targeted (by focusing on those who need help most). Yet both forms of support seek to address a common problem – that a minimum or living wage may not on its own be sufficient for all working households to reach an adequate standard of living.

Commentary

This chapter has considered interactions between wage levels and other factors influencing whether households have adequate income to live on. It has done so in the context of contemporary living and working patterns. Long-term trends such as the increase in the number of lone parent families and the growth of female and part-time employment have created a very different situation from when working families' main requirement was an adequate full-time male wage.

In this context, governments have to maintain a delicate balancing act in policies that set wages, working benefits and out of work benefits. In doing so, they have multiple objectives: to combat poverty, to preserve work incentives and reward work, and to maintain a healthy labour market. Setting out of work benefits too low will cause poverty and hardship. Setting them at a more generous level makes it relatively harder to maintain work incentives. But rather than basing such incentives on the "stick" of inadequate out-of-work benefits, a more constructive objective is to reward work through a combination of decent pay and income top-ups from the state, which bring living standards to a sufficient level for working families who are unable to reach such a standard only through their wages. This task can be made easier if the state can also help to bring work-related costs such as childcare down.

Getting the balance right between these policies affecting working households' living standards is today a crucial task for governments. In the

United Kingdom in recent years it can be argued that the balance went too far in favour of the state topping up low wages. Despite the introduction of a minimum wage in 1999, for the next decade a concerted effort by the Labour government to tackle child poverty saw billions being poured into tax credits while a cautious approach was taken to minimum wage setting, for fear of interfering unduly with the market. Ironically, it has been a Conservative government that has embarked on rebalancing this equation in favour of telling employers to pay more. But as it tests the limits to how high a compulsory wage floor can be set without it destroying large number of jobs, it must bear in mind that when this limit is reached, some families are bound still to need additional help from the state to make ends meet. Whether such a level can then genuinely be considered a "living wage" will depend in large part on whether such help is made available. In this way, the concept of a living wage can involve a rebalancing of responsibilities towards employers, but not an overbalancing in that direction. Any policy that seeks to enable all workers and their dependants to live on pay alone is bound to fail, in one of two ways. Either it will set a wage so high as to be unaffordable; or it will require some workers, with relatively heavy responsibilities for supporting families, to live in deep poverty.

5

Issues and choices for a sustainable living wage in the twenty-first century

While the term "living wage" sounds simple, this book has shown that both its interpretation and its application are far from straightforward.

The basic idea that we should organize society and the economy so that workers can earn enough to live a decent life remains highly pertinent today. As well as being the focus of numerous campaigns for better pay, it expresses a philosophical standpoint that makes excessive appropriation of wealth and income by the economically powerful, without considering the basic needs of workers, no more acceptable than when medieval Christians were writing about "just returns" for a worker's toil.

Applying this principle in a modern market economy is another matter entirely. Living wage campaigns achieved some remarkable victories in the late twentieth and early twenty-first centuries. Whether this will result in a generalized, permanent improvement in living conditions of low-paid workers depends on a wide range of factors. Some are related to political power, including the strength of living wage movements and the positions taken by political parties, influenced by public opinion. More fundamental are factors determining whether it is economically feasible in the long term to produce a sufficient number of jobs paying wages that support an acceptable standard of living, as defined by society. Governments cannot legislate such conditions simply by forbidding employers to pay less, although they can help foster them by contributing to workers' incomes or lowering their living costs through other subsidies, hence reducing the wage that a worker requires to be paid in order to produce a living income.

The future sustainability of the living wage cannot be taken for granted. It raises a range of issues, dilemmas and choices. This final chapter considers these under four broad headings, with a number of issues identified within each of them:

- Can the living wage remain true to its brand?
- How could the relationship between minimum and living wages develop?
- Who are the winners and losers from living wages?
- What will a living wage look like as work transforms?

Can the living wage remain true to its brand?

The imprecision of the term "living wage" can be both a strength and a weakness. It can be a strength because it makes it possible to adapt the application of the living wage to different conditions. It can be a weakness if the term becomes no more than a slogan or marketing tool, without having any real relationship to a worker's ability to maintain a given living standard. This raises issues about: how living wages are *measured*, how they are *uprated* and what *compromises* are accepted in keeping them affordable.

Measurement criteria matter

There is no single consistent way of calculating a living wage, but this does not mean that any method can equally well be used without consequence. Calculations based on reaching living standards already prevailing among relatively low income households, to represent current norms, to a large extent accept existing inequalities. Others that seek instead to measure actual needs can be oriented either to an "absolute" concept of human need or to one defined in relation to socially acceptable living standards that change with society. Which household types are used in the calculations also matters, for whether living wages seek to define a "family" living standard, or whether they are a benchmark based on what it takes to support an individual, relying on non-wage income to cover the additional needs of dependants. This is not however an "either–or" choice: most living wages try to some extent to meet family needs, but none are sufficient for a very large family.

One striking aspect of high profile living wage movements has been that the criteria used to set them have tended not to be much publicized or well understood. It would be unrealistic to think that the general public should have a close understanding of whatever formula is used. But a generic understanding of what a living wage seeks to represent can help reinforce long-term support for a living wage movement. For example, in the UK, the use of public deliberation to build consensus over what is an acceptable living standard has helped strengthen the "brand". It is hard to argue against the idea that wages should at least allow people to live at what the general public reckons to be a minimum acceptable standard.

How a living wage is uprated is crucial

In the 1930s, Franklin D. Roosevelt introduced a federal minimum wage to the United States, at a level deemed to be a "living wage", but later its value fell steeply both in absolute terms and relative to contemporary living standards. This shows that the achievement of getting a wage floor adopted can be diminished over time if there is no clear understanding of how its level will remain true to its original intention. Simply uprating it with inflation will not necessarily achieve this goal, if a living wage is related to a basket of goods and services whose contents may evolve over time with changes in society and with general living standards. One way of dealing with these changes can be to peg the wage to changes in average wages or incomes. Another is to continue to recalculate needs, taking account of changes in society.

While choosing a method of setting a living wage allows considerable discretion, its credibility rests on clarity and consistency in applying the method chosen

One reason why living wage calculation methods are not much discussed may be that campaigners are often conscious of operating within a narrow range between the unambitious and the unattainable. Set a living wage rate too low and it will do little to improve living standards; set it too high and it may never get adopted. The many different assumptions about household size, working hours and other factors that can go into a living wage calculation make it possible to select a method that operates within this range.

The fact that setting a living wage level may therefore allow considerable discretion does not however destroy its integrity. A living wage rate should at the very least derive from a consistent method, that in some way relates the wage to living costs and to a concept of a minimum living standard. Once established, as long as this consistency is maintained, a living wage can be seen as a benchmark sensitive to changes in living costs and living standards. Thus, while the rhetoric may refer to *the* living wage, one may more accurately think of *a* living wage as being one that has been accepted, in a particular place and context, as a consistent means of maintaining an agreed standard relating to living costs for the lowest paid workers.

How could the relationship between minimum and living wages develop?

At the end of Chapter 1, the distinction between minimum and living wages was shown to be a difficult one, because these two concepts are based on different aspects of wage floors: whether they are compulsory (minimum wages) and whether they are adequate (living wages). We have seen how, as living wage campaigns gain traction, there is a blurring of this distinction, insofar as public authorities accept the living wage argument as a reason for legislating a higher minimum. This raises the issues of whether distinguishing minimum and living wages is *feasible* and whether it is *desirable.*

Feasibility: minimum wages can never be wholly separate from or wholly identical to living wages

People arguing for and implementing minimum and living wages have sometimes consciously sought to keep them separate and at other times treated them as if they were the same. Some early social reformers felt that it was so important to legislate for a subsistence minimum to counter the inhuman conditions of sweatshops that arguing for a higher "living wage" through legislation would be counterproductive. More recently, statutory minimum wages have sometimes been explicitly worked out on economic criteria relating to labour markets, not living standards, being set at the level thought to avoid any threat to employment. Separately, living wage campaigns have sought to get private companies to pay living wages voluntarily where they can afford to, or to make them a requirement of public contracts, where there is arguably less of a risk of an adverse effect on labour demand than would be the case in a purely private context.

An underlying tension in this distinction is that compulsory minimum wages are bound ultimately to be motivated by the well-being of workers (or else why have them?), and hence can be criticized if they do not secure some decent standard of living. The desire to improve workers' living standards is behind pressure to increase minimum wage levels where they appear inadequate. Nevertheless, as seen in the United Kingdom, a government adopting the "living wage" label for a statutory minimum may be criticized by campaigners if this is not referenced to living standards, particularly if a true living wage is reckoned to be higher than the minimum set.

Desirability: could statutory adoption of a living wage be a poisoned chalice?

Given that living wage campaigns argue that paying workers less than they need to live on is ultimately immoral, should they regard statutory adoption of a living wage as the ultimate prize? In the United States, there may be little left for campaigns to do in states and cities that have adopted a $15 minimum for all employees, given that this is higher than most living wage ordinances applied to pubic contractors or taken up by other employers. In the United Kingdom, the compulsory "National Living Wage" (the minimum wage for over-25s) remains about £1 an hour below the voluntary rate outside London, but in 2016 the Labour Party's shadow chancellor, John McDonnell, promised to make a "real" living wage (taken to mean the accredited voluntary rate) compulsory if Labour were to come to power.

To do so may be a mixed blessing for the UK living wage movement, whose central organizer the Living Wage Foundation has never called for its living wage to become the minimum wage. It would at one level greatly increase the impact of this wage floor if it were applied to all workers, not just those whose employers voluntarily adopt it. Importantly, it would impact the lowest paying industries such as hotels and catering where there has been little take-up of this voluntary standard. It would also potentially make it easier for employers in such industries to pay more, knowing that competitors could not undercut them.

The big risk, however, is that once a living wage becomes compulsory, pressures to compromise on its level and coverage increase greatly. The risk of job losses resulting from forcing employers to pay a rate that is sensitive to living costs rather than focusing on what wages the market can sustain makes it unlikely that governments will stick with a formula truly designed to maintain an adequate living standard. There is also the temptation to allow a range of exemptions, of which the exclusion of under-25s from the official "National Living Wage" in the UK is a good example. The long-term decline in value of the US federal minimum demonstrates the value of continuing to set wage benchmarks outside the context of government, if only to maintain pressure to maintain the value of the statutory minimum. In the year after the introduction of the UK's "National Living Wage", voluntary accreditation for what is presented as the "real" living wage continued to grow. Yet its organizers tread a delicate path in responding to a higher but still inadequate compulsory minimum. At the very least, campaigners are bound to welcome increases in minimum wages that help achieve their objectives by obliging all employers – even if only for the time being and with exceptions – to pay something closer to a living wage rate.

Who are the winners and the losers from living wages?

Advocates understandably focus on the good news about the effects of living wages. There is no evidence that wage floors systematically reduce employment as predicted by neoclassical economic theory. The cost to an employer of paying higher wages can be offset by improved productivity and lower turnover of staff. There can also be a huge collective economic benefit of raising the morale and capabilities of the workforce, by reducing the hardship and stress experienced by workers with inadequate income.

Yet the idea that everyone gains from paying a living wage is much too simplistic. A living wage can involve redistribution of economic power, in a range of ways, not all of them predictable. Those who gain from it will sometimes, but not always, be workers in the greatest need. Governments can play an important role in influencing the outcomes of living wage policies. These issues are now considered in turn.

Living wages can redistribute economic power, not always in predictable ways

Some nineteenth-century writers regarded the total sum available for wages as fixed, and concluded that this made it impossible to make workers as a whole better off by setting a minimum. Today, in contrast, the respective shares of national income allocated to rewarding labour and providing returns on capital are recognized as variable, and indeed the French economist Thomas Piketty (2014) has shown that the share of capital is increasing over the long term and could continue to do so indefinitely. Much of this is related to the *accumulation* of capital, rather than to rates of return, but wage floors can help in a small way to redistribute income to labour from capital insofar as employers have been using market power to gain excessive rates of profit. Specifically, as discussed in Chapter 3, where workers have limited opportunities to switch jobs, wages can fall to a level below what firms could pay and still make an attractive return, in which cases raising minimum pay will transfer income directly from capital to labour.

The evidence shows, however, that there are many other potential consequences of wage floors. Over the long term, if labour becomes too expensive, eventually there will be an incentive to move to more capital-intensive modes of production (for example investing more in automated processes, using less labour and more machinery), reducing labour. Economic studies showing little employment effect may underestimate this long-term potential, since they tend to measure immediate effects, and also because the lack of such immediate job losses from modest increases may lead to bolder, higher wage floors. A shift from labour to capital inputs in response to higher pay *need* not make individual workers worse off if it takes the form of reduced hours rather than fewer jobs, but it is difficult to ensure that this is the case.

Even if the total amount of labour hired remains unchanged, a wage floor can produce winners and losers among the workforce. A weakening of collective bargaining on behalf of particular groups of workers, combined with the growing importance of setting general wage floors potentially changes the distribution of economic power. This may or may not work in favour of the least skilled, lowest paid workers.

One possibility is that it encourages a change in production methods to those utilizing greater skill levels, and that the lowest-paid workers who were meant to benefit lose out through substitution of workers with better skills, experience and productivity. The opposite effect is that less-skilled workers keep their jobs, whether because employers can afford to pay them more anyway or because they are encouraged to train them more, but this causes a flattening of pay structures in which better-paid staff lose out.

While such redistribution may be seen as part of the intention of living wages, it is important to distinguish whether the losers are, say, highly paid managers or, conversely, people with very modest pay such as supervisors. It is certainly far from inevitable that a living wage represents redistribution from rich to poor.

A further important way that living wages can redistribute economic well-being is through the price of goods and services. Price increases may be felt across the population, although overall where they derive from higher wages for the worst-off workers they are likely to be redistributive. Paying Asian garment workers enough to live on may increase clothing prices in Europe, but this will be redistributive globally. Paying hotel or restaurant workers more to provide basic services will be funded to a large degree by well-off consumers of these services – and while the low-paid workers who gain may also have to pay more for some things, this sharing of the cost should in principle mean that they come out ahead. What is harder to determine is the effect of rising costs where providers of publicly contracted services such as social care must pay their workers more. If these costs get passed on to the public authorities procuring the services, who work within fixed budgets, the quality and coverage of services could deteriorate. This can potentially hit lower income households more, because they are unable to provide for themselves where the state stops doing so.

People who gain most from being paid living wages are not systematically workers in the greatest need

Chapter 4 of this book established that although the lowest-paid workers are not all in the lowest-income households, there is nevertheless a substantial overlap between low pay and low income. This means that many of those who gain from living wages are indeed workers who are struggling to get by. However, the biggest beneficiaries are not necessarily those who struggle the most. For example, many of the lowest-paid jobs are done by young single people whose costs are lower than those of people supporting families.

Such comparisons need to be interpreted carefully in the context of the wage distribution and forms of social support in each country. In the United Kingdom, not only are young adults over-represented in the lowest-paying jobs, but they also are likely to pocket more of a wage increase than low-paid working families. This is because the latter are more often entitled to means-tested top-ups of their income, which they lose rapidly as earnings rise, offsetting the gains. One way of looking at this is that the gains from living wages are poorly targeted to people with high living costs. A different way is to see decent pay as being important precisely for those who do not have their living standards protected by the state. Single people are particularly vulnerable to the effects of very low pay because they have less social support to fall back on.

Governments' role in living wages goes well beyond deciding how high to set the statutory minimum

The above discussion has suggested that simply setting a wage floor can have unpredictable results. However, governments can play a crucial role in helping to influence such outcomes, in at least three ways.

First, as an employer, governments help set wage and employment practices. It can for example pioneer (or even legislate for) shorter working weeks that allow more sharing of work, to prevent any wage increase that reduces total employment from causing unemployment. Governments have also influenced pay structures, and so can influence the extent to which differentials are preserved when the minimum is raised, although it may prove costly to do so.

A second, related issue is whether the raising of a wage floor is matched by increased government spending to pay staff employed by the public sector or its contractors. For a government to require care workers to be paid a decent wage, to show that they are valued by society, is one thing. To raise the money needed to do so, without cutting services, is another. Raising taxes has never been popular. But doing so may ultimately be necessary as the other side of the morality of a living wage. If it is moral to pay a decent living to those who provide essential services, taxpayers may need to accept the moral case for funding it.

Third, governments can influence who ultimately gains from living wages through the ways that it supports low income households. While the direct effect of better pay may not accrue principally to workers who are already being compensated for low family income through tax credits, higher wage floors can make it more feasible to help these groups. Higher income tax revenues and a reduced need for means-tested support can both result from such wage increases, making it more affordable for governments to be generous in paying family benefits. In the long term, a society that provides more adequate market rewards is better able to afford a decent safety net for people facing hard times – whether in the form of reduced income from work or becoming unemployed.

What will a living wage look like as work transforms?

In 1930, the economist John Maynard Keynes predicted that by 2030, technology and productivity would have advanced to such a level that everyone could satisfy their needs by working three hours a day for five days a week (Keynes [1930] 1963). While rumours of the imminent death of hard work have been frequently exaggerated, forecasts of a largely roboticized world with a declining need for labour continue to resurface with today's economists (e.g. Sachs & Kotlikoff 2012). Unlike Keynes, however, they recognize that even a huge rise in the productive capacity of the economy has not caused people, even the rich, to feel that they have all that they need so there is no point acquiring more. This may help explain why work and wealth are not being shared in the way that Keynes had hoped. Rather, as the importance of capital grows, it also becomes increasingly concentrated, as does the income that it generates (Piketty 2014). While a dystopian vision of a world run by robots is at worst a long way off, automation has already had many casualties, and economies have not been good at distributing the fruits of technologically driven growth across the workforce.

This raises the underlying issue of how the payment of a living wage can remain economically viable over the long term. The more expensive labour becomes relative to automated alternatives, the greater the incentive to replace it with machines. One reason it could be argued that this is not too serious a problem at present in western countries is that the vast majority of jobs are in services rather than manufacturing, and that many service jobs are relatively hard to automate. Yet this argument is rapidly weakening, not just with automation of such functions as supermarket checkouts, but also with the introduction of robots into intensely personal fields such as social care. Arguing that people prefer to be served by human beings cuts little ice with those delivering public services under impossibly tight budgets or companies facing severe price competition. A different argument, that people need to work in order to be fulfilled and feel valued, as well as to help distribute income, suggests interventions that override what the market on its own will deliver.

The difficulty in spreading wealth across society in an emerging world where much production is generated from capital held by a small number of people has been an important reason why the concept of a "universal basic income" has become popular in recent years. Paying everyone a certain sum that they could live on at a basic level, it is argued, may become the only way of distributing income across society in the absence of well-paying jobs for all. The two biggest political obstacles to such a proposition are the need to finance it, potentially by taxing the better-off at very high rates, and popular resistance to the idea that people should get "something for nothing" (see Hirsch 2015). On the other hand, if the economics of a living wage were to transform to the point where demand for labour was insufficient to create jobs even at a level sufficient to sustain a single person, some combination of living wage and universal basic income may become attractive. Under this scenario, a state-provided income for each citizen would provide a building block towards an adequate living standard, but earning a living wage set at a level that the market could sustain would also be required. This would help maintain work incentives and the fulfilment that people gain from working.

In practice, the willingness of taxpayers to support any kind of unconditional basic income remains a long way off. However, even today, state entitlements often combine with wage floors to determine whether families can make ends meet. In the future, living wages can continue to play an important role, if they are coordinated with other policies to ensure that workers feel valued by society, and that they can enjoy a socially acceptable standard of living.

References

Addison, J., M. Blackburn & C. Cotti 2013. "Minimum Wage Increases in a Recessionary Environment". *Labour Economics* **23**: 30–39.

Anker, R. 2011. *Estimating a Living Wage: A Methodological Review*. Geneva: International Labour Organization.

Aquinas, T. 1265–74. *Summa Theologiae*, part I-II, question 114, article 1. Retrieved from www.newadvent.org/summa/2114.htm (accessed 12 January 2017).

Belman, D. & P. Wofson 2014. *What Does the Minimum Wage Do?* Kalamazoo, MI: W. E. Upjohn Institute for Employment Research.

Bennett, F. 2014. "The 'Living Wage', Low Pay and In-Work Poverty: Rethinking the Relationships". *Critical Social Policy* **34**(1): 46–65.

Bernstein, J. 2004. "The Living Wage Movement: What Is it, Why Is it, and What's Known About its Impact?" In *Emerging Labor Market Institutions for the Twenty-First Century*, R. Freeman, J. Hersch & L. Mishel (eds), 99–140. Chicago, IL: University of Chicago Press.

Beveridge, W. 1942. *National Insurance and Allied Services*. London: Her Majesty's Stationery Office.

Bhatia, R. & M. Katz 2001. "Estimation of Health Benefits from a Local Living Wage Ordinance". *American Journal of Public Health* **91**: 1398–402.

Blackburn, S. 2007. "Must Low Pay Always Be with Us? The Origins of Britain's Minimum Wage Legislation". *Historical Studies in Industrial Relations* **23/24**: 214–39.

Booth, C. 1889. *Life and Labour of the People*, vol. I. London: Williams & Norgate.

Bourne, R. 2015. "Do Tax Credits 'Subsidise' Employers?". Retrieved from www.iea.org.uk/blog/do-tax-credits-%E2%80%98subsidise%E2%80%99-employers#comment-14384 (accessed 23 August 2016).

Brenner, M. 2004. *The Economic Impact of Living Wage Ordinances*. Working paper. Amherst, MA: Political Economy Research Institute.

Brewer, M., R. May & D. Phillips 2009. *Taxes, Benefits and the National Minimum Wage*. London: Institute for Fiscal Studies.

Brown, W., A. Bryson & J. Forth 2008. *Competition and the Retreat from Collective Bargaining*. Discussion paper no. 318. London: National Institute of Economic and Social Research.

Cahuc, P., S. Carcillo, U. Rinne & K. F. Zimmermann 2013. "Youth Unemployment in Old Europe: The Polar Cases of France and Germany". *IZA Journal of European Labor Studies* **2**: 18.

Card, D. & A. Krueger 1994. "A Case Study of the Fast-Food Industry in New Jersey and Pennsylvania". *American Economic Review* **84**(4): 772–93.

Card, D. & A. Krueger 1998. *A Reanalysis of the Effect of the New Jersey Minimum Wage Increase on the Fast-Food Industry with Representative Payroll Data*. Working paper 6386. Cambridge, MA: National Bureau of Economic Research.

Card, D. & A. Krueger 2000. "A Case Study for the Fast-Food Industry in New Jersey and Pennsylvania: Reply". *American Economic Review* **90**(5): 1397–420.

Card, D. & A. Krueger 2016. *Myth and Measurement: The New Economics of the Minimum Wage*. Princeton, NJ: Princeton University Press.

Churchill, W. 1909. Speech introducing Trades Boards Bill. 28 April. *Hansard* series 5, vol. 4, col. 38.

CIPD 2016. *Weighing up the Wage Floor: Employer Responses to the National Living Wage*. London: Resolution Foundation.

Ciscel, D. 2002. "The Determination of Living Wage". In *Living Wage Movements: Global Perspectives*, D. M. Figart (ed.), 51–66. New York: Routledge.

Clark, G. 2007. "The Long March of History: Farm Wages, Population, and Economic Growth, England 1209–1869". *Economic History Review* **60**(1): 97–135.

D'Arcy, C. & D. Finch 2016. *Calculating a Living Wage for London and the Rest of the UK*. London: Resolution Foundation.

Davis, A., D. Hirsch, M. Padley & L. Marshall 2015. *How Much is Enough? Reaching Social Consensus on Minimum Household Needs*. Loughborough: Centre for Research in Social Policy.

Dickson, M. & K. Papps 2016. *How the National Minimum Wage Affects Flows In and Out of Employment: An Investigation Using Worker-Level Data*. London: Low Pay Commission.

Dolado, J., F. Kramarz, S. Machin, A. Manning, D. Margolis & C. Teuling 1996. "The Economic Impact of Minimum Wages in Europe". *Economic Policy* **11**(23): 317–72.

Dube, A. 2013. "Minimum Wages and the Distribution of Family Incomes". Retrieved from https://dl.dropboxusercontent.com/u/15038936/Dube_MinimumWagesFamilyIncomes.pdf (accessed 5 October 2016).

Dube, A., W. Lester & M. Reich 2010. "Minimum Wage Effects Across State Borders: Estimates Using Continuous Counties". *Review of Economics and Statistics* **92**(4): 945–64.

Economic Policy Institute 2015. *The Economic Policy Institute's 2015 Family Budget Calculator: Technical Documentation.* Working paper 299. Washington, DC: Economic Policy Institute.

Fairris, D., D. Runsten, C. Briones & J. Goodheart 2015. *Examining the Evidence: The Impact of the Los Angeles Living Wage Ordinance on Workers and Businesses.* Los Angeles, CA: Institute for Research on Labor and Employment, UCLA. Retrieved from http://escholarship.org/uc/item/0b73b6f0 (accessed 17 October 2016).

Flint, E., S. Cummins & J. Wills 2013. "Investigating the Effect of the London Living Wage on the Psychological Wellbeing of Low-Wage Service Sector Employees: A Feasibility Study". *Journal of Public Health* **36**(2):187–93.

Gonzalez Güemez, I. 1997. "Los efectos del salario mínimo sobre el empleo de adolescentes, jóvenes y mujeres: evidencia empírica para el caso español". *Cuadernos Económicos de ICE* **63**: 31–48.

Gorry, A. 2013. "Minimum Wages and Youth Unemployment". *European Economic Review* **64**: 57–75.

Greenhouse, S. & J. Kasperkevic 2015. "Fight for $15 Swells into Largest Protest by Low-Wage Workers in US History". *The Guardian* (15 April). Retrieved from www.theguardian.com/us-news/2015/apr/15/fight-for-15-minimum-wage-protests-new-york-los-angeles-atlanta-boston (accessed 4 January 2017).

Hindustan Times 2016. "Govt Panel Fails to Define 'Poverty Line', Says Form Another Group to Do the Job". *Hindustan Times* (12 September). Retrieved from www.hindustantimes.com/india-news/a-govt-panel-on-poverty-doesn-t-know-what-it-is/story-bsPvj90skcTbKJRFdxtAsM.html (accessed 14 October 2016).

Hirsch, D. 2015. *Could a Citizen's Income Work?* York: Joseph Rowntree Foundation.

Howes, C. 2002. *The Impact of a Large Wage Increase on the Workforce Stability of IHSS Home Care Workers in San Francisco County.* Working paper. Berkeley, CA: Institute for Research on Labor and Employment.

Immervoll, H. 2007. *Minimum Wages, Minimum Labour Costs and the Tax Treatment of Low-Wage Employment.* IZA paper 2555. Bonn: Institute for the Study of Labour.

Joseph Rowntree Foundation 2016. *UK Poverty: Causes, Costs and Solutions.* York: Joseph Rowntree Foundation

Kahn-Freund, O. 1968. *Labour Law: Old Traditions and New Developments.* Toronto: Clarke, Irwin.

Keynes, J. M. [1930] 1963. "Economic Possibilities for our Grandchildren". In his *Essays in Persuasion*, 358–73. New York: Norton.

King, P. & C. Waldegrave 2012. *Report of an Investigation into Defining a Living Wage for New Zealand.* Wellington: Family Centre Social Policy Research Unit.

Lawton, K. & M. Pennycook 2013. *Beyond the Bottom Line: The Challenges and Opportunities of a Living Wage*. London: IPPR & Resolution Foundation.

Lemos, S. 2008. "A Survey of the Effects of the Minimum Wage on Prices". *Journal of Economic Surveys* 22(1): 187–212.

Leo XIII, Pope 1891. *Rerum Novarum: On Capital and Labour*. Vatican City: Libreria Editrice Vaticana.

Levin-Waldman, O. 2005. *The Political Economy of the Living Wage*. Armonk, NY: M. E. Sharpe.

Living Wage Commission 2016. *Closing the Gap: A Living Wage that Means Families Don't Go Short*. London: Living Wage Foundation.

Low Pay Commission 2016. *National Minimum Wage, Low Pay Commission Report Spring 2016*. London: Low Pay Commission.

Luce, S. 2005. "Lessons from Living-Wage Campaigns". *Work and Occupations* 32(4): 423–40.

Machin, S., A. Manning & L. Rahman 2003. "Where the Minimum Wage Bites Hard: Introduction of Minimum Wages to a Low Wage Sector". *Journal of the European Economic Association* 1: 154–80.

Maitre, B., B. Nolan & C. Whelan 2012. "Low Pay, In-Work Poverty and Economic Vulnerability: A Comparative Analysis Using EU-SILC". *The Manchester School* 80(1): 99–116.

Marshall, A. 1895. *Principles of Economics*, 3rd edn. London: Macmillan.

Marx, I. & K. Nelson (eds) 2013. *Minimum Income Protection in Flux*. London: Palgrave Macmillan.

Marx, K. [1849] 1972. *Wage Labour and Capital*. In *The Marx–Engels Reader*, R. C. Tucker (ed.), 203–17. Princeton, NJ: Princeton University Press.

Marx, K. [1885] 1977. *Capital, Volume 2*. New York: International Publishers.

Metcalf, D. 2008. "Why has the British National Minimum Wage had Little or No Impact on Employment?" *Journal of Industrial Relations* 50(3): 489–512.

Mill, J. S. [1909] 1969. *Principles of Political Economy*. New York: Augustus M. Kelley.

Neumark, D. & W. Wascher 1995. *The Effect of New Jersey's Minimum Wage Increase on Fast-Food Employment: A Re-evaluation Using Payroll Records*. Working paper 5224. Cambridge, MA: National Bureau for Economic Research.

Neumark, D. & W. Wascher 2000. "Minimum Wages and Employment: A Case Study of the Fast-Food Industry in New Jersey and Pennsylvania: Comment". *American Economic Review* 90(5): 1362–96.

Neumark, D. & W. Wascher 2008. *Minimum Wages*. Cambridge, MA: MIT Press.

Nolan, B. & I. Marx 2000. "Low Pay and Household Poverty". In *Labour Market Inequalities: Problems and Policies of Low-Wage Employment in International Perspective*, M. Gregory, W. Salverda & S. Bazen (eds), 100–119. Oxford: Oxford University Press.

OECD 2015. *Focus on Minimum Wages After the Crisis: Making them Pay*. Paris: OECD.

Office for Budget Responsibility 2015. *Economic and Fiscal Outlook July 2015*. London: Office for Budget Responsibility.

Oldroyd, M. 1894. *A Living Wage*. Leeds: McCorquodale.

Osborne, G. 2015. "Chancellor George Osborne's Summer Budget 2015 Speech". 8 July. Retrieved from www.gov.uk/government/speeches/chancellor-george-osbornes-summer-budget-2015-speech (accessed 12 January 2017).

Pereira, S. 2003. "The Impact of Minimum Wages on Youth Employment in Portugal". *European Economic Review* 47: 229–44.

Perez Dominguez, C. 1995. "Los efectos del salario mínimo sobre el empleo y el desempleo: Evidencia empírica para España". In *Actas de las Primera Jornadas de Economía Laboral*, 1–13. Alcalá de Henares: Universidad de Alcalá de Henares. Retrieved from www.researchgate.net/publication/257609477_Los_efectos_del_salario_minimo_sobre_el_empleo_y_el_desempleo_evidencia_empirica_para_Espana_Actas_de_las_Primeras_Jornadas_de_Economia_Laboral_Alcala_de_Heneres (accessed 4 January 2017).

Perez Dominguez, C. & I. Gonzalez Güemez 2005. "Salario mínimo, mercado de trabajo y promesas electorales". *Revista universitaria de ciencias del trabajo* 6: 59–81.

Piketty, T. 2014. *Capital in the Twenty-First Century*. Cambridge, MA: Harvard University Press.

Pollin, R. & S. Luce 1998. *The Living Wage: Building a Fair Economy*. New York: The New Press.

Richards, T., M. Cohen, S. Klein & D. Littman 2008. *Working for a Living Wage: Making Paid Work Meet Basic Family Needs in Vancouver and Victoria*. Vancouver: Centre for Policy Alternatives.

Roosevelt, F. D. 1933. "Franklin Roosevelt's Statement on the National Industrial Recovery Act". 16 June. retrieved from http://docs.fdrlibrary.marist.edu/odnirast.html (accessed 12 January 2017).

Rosenheim, N. 2015. "The Historic Legacy of the Food-Income Poverty Model". 17 November. Retrieved from https://apafig.wordpress.com/tag/thrifty-food-plan (accessed 13 October 2016).

Rowntree, B. S. 1901. *Poverty: A Study of Town Life*. London: Macmillan.

Ryan, J. 1912. *A Living Wage: Its Ethical and Economic Aspects*. London: Macmillan.

Sachs, J. & L. Kotlikoff 2012. *Smart Machines and Long-Term Misery*. Working paper 18629. Cambridge, MA: National Bureau for Economic Research.

Schmitt, J. 2013. *Why Does the Minimum Wage Have No Discernible Effect on Employment?* Working paper. Washington, DC: Center for Economic and Policy Research.

Select Committee of the House of Lords on the Sweating System 1888–9. *Fifth Report from the Select Committee of the House of Lords on the Sweating System*. London: Hansard.

Siders, D. 2016. "Jerry Brown Signs $15 Minimum Wage in California". *Sacramento Bee* (4 April). Retrieved from www.sacbee.com/news/politics-government/capitol-alert/article69842317.html (accessed 12 January 2017).

Smith, A. 1776. *An Enquiry Into the Nature and Causes of the Wealth of Nations*. London: W. Strahan & T. Cadell. Page numbers cited in the text refer to the undated edition freely downloadable from www.ifaarchive.com/pdf/smith_-_an_inquiry_into_the_nature_and_causes_of_the_wealth_of_nations%5B1%5D. pdf (accessed 3 January 2017).

Stabile, D. 2008. *The Living Wage: Lessons from the History of Economic Thought*. Cheltenham: Elgar.

Stewart, M. & J. Swaffield 2002. "Using the BHPS Wave 9 Additional Questions to Evaluate the Impact of the National Minimum Wage". *Oxford Bulletin of Economics and Statistics* **64**: 633–52.

Stewart, M. & J. Swaffield 2004. *The Other Margin: Do Minimum Wages Cause Working Hours Adjustments for Low-Wage Workers?* London: Low Pay Commission.

Townsend, P. 1979. *Poverty in the United Kingdom*. London: Penguin.

Tyson, L. d'A. 2013. "Raising the Minimum Wage: Old Shibboleths, New Evidence". *The New York Times* (13 December). Retrieved from http://mobile.nytimes.com/blogs/economix/2013/12/13/raising-the-minimum-wage-old-shibboleths-new-evidence/?smid=tw-share (accessed 4 January 2017).

Wadsworth, J. 2007. *Did the Minimum Wage Change Consumption Patterns? Report to Low Pay Commission*. Working paper 1517. London: Centre for Economic Performance.

Wilkinson, F. 2001. "The Theory and Practice of Wage Subsidisation: Some Historical Reflections". In *The Employment Tax Credit and the Future of In-Work Support*, F. Bennett & D. Hirsch (eds), 94–125. York: Joseph Rowntree Foundation.

Wills, J. & B. Linneker 2012. *The Costs and Benefits of the London Living Wage*. London: Queen Mary University of London.

Winter, J. M. & D. M. Joslin (eds) 1972. *R. H. Tawney's Commonplace Book*. Cambridge: Cambridge University Press.

Index